IMAGES
of America

REMEMBERING
KENTUCKY'S
CONFEDERATES

Jefferson Davis was born on June 3, 1808, in what was then known as Christian County, Kentucky. The location is now the Jefferson Davis State Historic Site near Fairview in Todd County. Davis moved to Mississippi as a child and had an illustrious military and political career, graduating from West Point and serving with distinction in the Mexican War. When secession loomed, Davis returned to Mississippi, was elected president of the Confederate States of America, and served four years as the Confederacy's only president. He was captured while attempting to flee the country in May 1865 and imprisoned to await trial for treason. Released in 1867, Davis returned home to Mississippi, but he never forgot his origins in Kentucky, which he described as "my own, my native land." (Gary Gardner.)

ON THE COVER: This battle flag of the 4th Kentucky Infantry was carried in 1862 and was taken back to Kentucky following the end of the war. (Waveland State Historic Site.)

IMAGES
of America

REMEMBERING KENTUCKY'S CONFEDERATES

Geoffrey R. Walden

ARCADIA
PUBLISHING

Published by Arcadia Publishing
Charleston, South Carolina

Library of Congress Catalog Card Number: 2008927847

For all general information contact Arcadia Publishing at:
Telephone 843-853-2070
Fax 843-853-0044
E-mail sales@arcadiapublishing.com
For customer service and orders:
Toll-Free 1-888-313-2665

Visit us on the Internet at www.arcadiapublishing.com

This book is dedicated to the memory of my great-great-great uncle Amos Worrell Pence of the 8th Kentucky Cavalry CSA and to Robert H. Lindsay, color-bearer of the 4th Kentucky Infantry CSA, who was twice named to the Confederate Roll of Honor and who carried the colors in all of his regiment's battles until his death in action at Jonesboro, Georgia, in August 1864.

CONTENTS

ACKNOWLEDGMENTS

This book is a compilation of photographs from all across Kentucky and the United States. A subject such as this, with no single large collection from which to draw, could not have been completed without the significant assistance of several individuals. My friend and colleague Tim Bowman of the Sons of Confederate Veterans not only donated photographs for the book but put me in touch with several collectors who helped with images. I am greatly indebted to the work of the late Porter Harned, founder of the Orphan Brigade Kinfolk, who spent over 20 years gathering photographs of Kentucky Confederates. Without the cheerful assistance of Alice Bratcher, secretary-treasurer of the Orphan Brigade Kinfolk, this book would have not been possible.

Sam Flora of the Morgan's Men Association and Billy and Barry Byrd of the Octagon Hall Museum were very helpful with images from those collections. I wish to thank Sandy Staebell and Nancy Baird for permitting me to use images from the collections of the Kentucky Library, Western Kentucky University. Jason Flahardy of the University of Kentucky Special Collections and Bill Bright and Charlene Smith of the Kentucky Historical Society made photographs from those collections available. Gary Gardner, Joey Oller, Jordan Ricketts, Mike Sisk, and Mickey Storms of the Sons of Confederate Veterans provided several valuable images.

I wish to sincerely thank all of those who donated images of their Confederate relatives for use in this book; they are acknowledged in the caption credit lines. During the collection of photographs for this book, several previously unknown gems came to light. One of these is the cover image, which was provided by Chris Propes of the Waveland State Historic Site.

Luke Cunningham, my editor at Arcadia, had the original idea for this book, and his encouragement helped bring the project to fruition.

Last but far from least, I wish to thank my wife Deborah and daughter Erin for indulging me during family vacations with all of those side trips to visit yet another Civil War site—they have made my history explorations so much more enjoyable.

INTRODUCTION

The Civil War in Kentucky was truly a conflict of "brother against brother." As a border state, the commonwealth was divided in sentiment, which was perhaps best expressed by Phil Lee of Shepherdsville, who would later command the 2nd Kentucky Infantry: he was for the Union, but should the Union be dissolved, he was for Kentucky; if Kentucky was dissolved, he was for Bullitt County; if Bullitt County dissolved, he was for Shepherdsville; and if Shepherdsville dissolved, he was for his side of the street.

This division of sentiment and loyalties led Kentuckians who supported the Confederacy to form units and volunteer for the Southern cause. Some 35 regiments of infantry and cavalry and batteries of artillery served in the Confederate forces from Kentucky. Undoubtedly the most famous of these were the 1st Kentucky Brigade, known to history as the "Orphan Brigade," and Gen. John Hunt Morgan's cavalry command.

The nucleus of the 1st Kentucky Brigade was formed in September 1861. Following a brief period of service around Bowling Green, Kentucky, the brigade left the state in early 1862 and never returned during the war. Because the soldiers were exiled from their native state and cut off from families at home, they came to view themselves as "orphans" whose only home was the Confederate army. After losing two of their brigade commanders in battle, they began to call themselves the "Orphan Brigade."

The Orphan Brigade fought all across the South in the western theater of war, from Kentucky to Louisiana, Mississippi, Tennessee, Georgia, and South Carolina. They participated in most of the major battles of the Confederate Army of Tennessee, earning a reputation for steadiness in battle and unequaled prowess in drill. Following the Atlanta Campaign of 1864, the Orphans were converted to mounted infantry. By the end of the war, they were located in South Carolina, where the 4th Kentucky Infantry fought one of the last actions east of the Mississippi River on April 29, 1865. The survivors of the Orphan Brigade were paroled at Washington, Georgia, on May 6–7, 1865.

John Hunt Morgan, a native of Lexington, formed a regiment of cavalry volunteers in late 1861. These men served with the 1st Kentucky Brigade, fighting beside one another at the famous Battle of Shiloh, Tennessee, in April 1862. Morgan's Men then became an independent command of partisan rangers, who specialized in operating behind enemy lines and disrupting transportation, supply, and communications lines. Morgan raided behind enemy lines into Kentucky on four main occasions, but his most famous exploit was the "Great Raid" into Indiana and Ohio in the summer of 1863. Although the raid ended in the capture of Morgan and most of his men, they managed to keep several Northern units occupied and away from the main battle lines in Tennessee and Mississippi.

Other Confederate units and soldiers from Kentucky fought on nearly every battlefield of the War, including Gettysburg, Sharpsburg, and fields in Alabama, North Carolina, Virginia, and the mountains of eastern Kentucky and western Virginia. Kentucky soldiers fought to the last and formed the escort for Confederate president Jefferson Davis when he attempted to flee the country in May 1865.

Kentucky's Confederates who returned home in 1865 did not face the same level of destruction as soldiers from some other Southern states, but harsh Union measures taken against guerrilla fighters in 1864 and 1865 had turned public opinion against the Federal military. As time went on after the Kentucky soldiers returned home, it came to be a badge of honor to be counted among the state's Confederate veterans. Reunions were popular for several years, and Kentuckians were active in marking their units' positions and activities on various battlefields. These monuments, along with fading photographs such as those in this book, continue to remind us of the valor and fortitude possessed by the Kentuckians who left their homes to fight for Southern independence.

Several Internet pages on the World Wide Web contain more information on Kentucky Confederates. Two of these are the 1st Kentucky "Orphan" Brigade Homepage, www.rootsweb. ancestry.com/~orphanhm/index.html, and the Morgan's Men Association Homepage, members. tripod.com/~Morgans_Men/.

Many wonderful photographs of Kentucky Confederates came to light during the compilation of this book. Many more doubtless remain to be discovered and published. Anyone who has an image of a Kentucky Confederate, such as those seen here, who would be willing to share it for a possible future work, is encouraged to contact the author at geoff_walden@hotmail.com or in care of the publisher.

One

KENTUCKIANS
PREPARE FOR WAR

Many Kentucky Confederate units had their origins in the Kentucky State Guard, the state militia. The militia underwent reorganization and modernization in 1860, which culminated in a weeklong encampment in Louisville called Camp Boone. The State Guard companies, which each had a distinctive uniform, gathered at the fair grounds to pitch their tents and drill in formation. (*Sketches of Camp Boone*, 1860.)

Simon Bolivar Buckner of Hart County commanded the Kentucky State Guard. Buckner designed uniforms of cadet gray color with distinctive rank insignia for himself and his staff. Photographs like this one were widely published in the North, and many assumed that this was the Confederate uniform in 1861. Early images of many Confederate generals, hastily published in the North, have this uniform drawn onto the subjects. (*Sketches of Camp Boone*, 1860.)

A majority of the members of the Kentucky State Guard held Southern sympathies, and several companies went south in the summer of 1861 to join the fledgling Confederacy. In this photograph, Kentucky governor Beriah Magoffin meets with Thomas Hunt, major of the Louisville Battalion. Hunt later commanded the 9th Kentucky Infantry of the famous Orphan Brigade. (*Sketches of Camp Boone*, 1860.)

Frank P. Tryon of Louisville served as the assistant quartermaster of the Kentucky State Guard. In July 1861, he was commissioned as a lieutenant in the 2nd Kentucky Infantry of the Orphan Brigade. Tryon was mortally wounded at the Battle of Murfreesboro on January 2, 1863, and fell into the hands of the enemy. He died in a Federal hospital in Nashville on January 9. (*Sketches of Camp Boone*, 1860.)

Kentucky governor Beriah Magoffin and his wife (fifth and sixth from left) visit Col. Frank Tryon (seventh from left), assistant quartermaster of the Kentucky State Guard. Several varieties of State Guard uniforms can be seen in this photograph. Some State Guard companies wore gray, some regulation blue, some dressed in "hunting shirts" like their pioneer forebears, and some wore the latest military fashion. (*Sketches of Camp Boone*, 1860.)

Capt. Philip Vacaro of Louisville served as chief of the Subsistence Department of the Kentucky State Guard. In October 1861, he joined Company B of the 9th Kentucky Infantry under Col. Thomas Hunt, his old superior in the Kentucky State Guard. He was appointed captain and served in the Confederate Commissary Department. Vacaro is buried in his family plot in Cave Hill Cemetery in Louisville. (*Sketches of Camp Boone, 1860.*)

Maj. Thomas Hunt is seen again in this view on the left of the group of officers at the right. This State Guard company was the Citizen Guards of Louisville, resplendent in their tall bearskin hats. Their knapsacks, which can be seen leaning against their stacked muskets, carried the designation "C.G." painted on the back. Many of these men later joined the 9th Kentucky Infantry. (*Sketches of Camp Boone, 1860.*)

John Hunt Morgan of Lexington, a veteran of the war with Mexico, raised and commanded a militia company called the Lexington Rifles. Morgan went on to become one of the most famous Confederate cavalry commanders before his death in 1864. This image shows him early in the war when he commanded a cavalry squadron. (Waveland State Historic Site.)

Morgan's Lexington Rifles were accepted for service in the Kentucky State Guard, and this image from Camp Boone in 1860 shows their company street. The Rifles elicited the admiration of the local populace with their drills and shooting exhibitions. Some of the Rifles wore a uniform patterned after the hunting shirts of their frontiersmen forebears, while others wore a dark green frock coat and shako hat. (*Sketches of Camp Boone*, 1860.)

Beyond doubt, the most famous Kentuckian to join the Southern ranks was John Cabell Breckinridge of Lexington. A former vice president of the United States and presidential candidate in the 1860 election, Breckinridge threw his lot in with the South when Kentucky abandoned neutrality. Beloved by his men, he rose to the rank of major general and secretary of war in the Confederate government. (Special Collections, University of Kentucky.)

Delegates from all over Kentucky met in Russellville in November 1861 to discuss secession, voting to form a separate state government. Kentucky was admitted as a state in the Confederacy on December 10, 1861, and adopted this state seal, showing a mailed arm representing Kentucky offering a 13th star to the 12 Confederate states. (*Proceedings of the Convention Establishing Provisional Government of Kentucky*, 1863.)

Two

KENTUCKY CONFEDERATE INFANTRY SOLDIERS

Pvt. James Armistead Guthrie Churchill was born in Calloway County in 1836. He served in Company F of the 1st Kentucky Infantry along the Potomac River line in Northern Virginia. When the regiment was disbanded in the spring of 1862, Churchill joined Woodward's 2nd Kentucky Cavalry. In this image Churchill wears a Kentucky-style pleated-front frock coat. (Orphan Brigade Kinfolk.)

Clinton Augustus Lewis enlisted in the "Davis' Rangers," Company H, 1st Kentucky Infantry. He served with this regiment in Northern Virginia, fighting in the Battle of Dranesville on December 20, 1861. When the regiment's enlistment was up in the spring of 1862, Lewis traveled to Tennessee to enlist in the 2nd Kentucky Cavalry. See page 77. (Orphan Brigade Kinfolk.)

Two Confederate comrades from Kentucky posed for this photograph while they were prisoners of war at Camp Douglas in Chicago. On the left is Montgomery Merritt, who served in Company K, 1st Kentucky Infantry, and Company G, 3rd/7th Kentucky Cavalry. Merritt posed for his portrait with Frank G. Browder of the 3rd/7th Kentucky Cavalry. (Orphan Brigade Kinfolk.)

Simon Bolivar Buckner left his command in the Kentucky State Guard to accept a commission in the Confederate army. In this image, he posed wearing the uniform he had designed for his State Guard officers, a frock coat of cadet gray color with distinctive collar and shoulder insignia. This uniform coat is preserved today in the Museum of the Confederacy in Richmond, Virginia. (Special Collections, University of Kentucky.)

As a Confederate general, Simon B. Buckner designed this pleated-front frock coat, which is said to be inspired by the hunting shirts of Kentucky frontiersmen. A popular style with Confederate officers, when Gen. Leonidas Polk saw it he exclaimed, "I like it, sir, it looks comfortable, it looks soldierly, in fact, sir, it looks rebellious!" This coat can be seen today in the Museum of the Confederacy. (Timothy D. Bowman.)

Fayette Hewitt, one of the most admired Kentucky Confederates, was born in Hardin County in 1831. In 1863, he was assigned as assistant adjutant general of the Kentucky Orphan Brigade and remained in that position for the rest of the war. Hewitt refused to accept promotion because he said he would rather remain a Kentucky captain than be a general in any other brigade. (Timothy D. Bowman.)

Recording in his journal that he could not resist his country's call, James E. Paton (or Patton) enlisted in Company G ("Hamilton Guards") of the 2nd Kentucky Infantry. He was captured with the rest of his regiment when the Confederate force at Fort Donelson surrendered in February 1862. In this image he is seen wearing the distinctive uniform of the Hamilton Guards. (Blue Grass Trust for Historic Preservation.)

John Washington Payne joined the Confederate army in July 1861 from Frankfort, Kentucky. He served as chief bugler of the 2nd Kentucky Infantry, fighting at Fort Donelson, Hartsville, Murfreesboro, Chickamauga, and other battles of his command. Payne posed for this ambrotype image early in the war, holding his bugle and wearing a kepi with brass letters. He died in Frankfort in 1883. (HA.com.)

Bugler John W. Payne of the 2nd Kentucky Infantry captured this battered bugle from the Federals at the battle of Hartsville, Tennessee, on December 7, 1862. This prize was engraved with Confederate battle flags and the names of several battles. After the war, Payne continued to play this bugle at Orphan Brigade reunions, and it is displayed today in the Kentucky Military History Museum in Frankfort. (Geoff Walden.)

"A good soldier from first to last," James H. Gregory of Falmouth enlisted in July 1861, in Company F, 2nd Kentucky Infantry. He fought at Fort Donelson and was surrendered with his regiment. When the Atlanta Campaign began, Gregory fought at Resaca and Dallas, Georgia, where he was killed at the front of his company in an assault on the enemy's works on May 28, 1864. (*Confederate Veteran Association*, 1895.)

David Osborn was born in Scott County in 1841 and joined Company H, 2nd Kentucky Infantry in 1861. Osborn fought at Fort Donelson in February 1862, where he was slightly wounded. The 2nd Kentucky Infantry successfully defended their section of the earthworks, but the garrison was surrendered and the men went into prisoner of war camps. Osborn died in 1905 and was buried in the Florence Cemetery. (Dave Osborn.)

Philip Lightfoot Lee was born in Bullitt County on October 22, 1832. In 1861, he chose to fight for "his side of the street" (see page 7) and joined the 2nd Kentucky Infantry. He was promoted to colonel in 1864 and commanded his regiment for the remainder of the war. When Lee died in July 1875, the flag on Louisville's city hall was lowered to half-mast. (*History of the Orphan Brigade*, 1898.)

Lexington native Marnix W. Virden enlisted in Company B, 2nd Kentucky Infantry at the age of 17. He was wounded in nearly every battle he fought. During the Orphan Brigade's attack against Federal breastworks at Chickamauga on September 20, 1863, Virden lost his right leg. He was named to the Confederate Roll of Honor for his gallant conduct on that field. (*Confederate Veteran Association*, 1895.)

Sgt. Vivian Crosthwaite served from Warren County, Kentucky, joining Company C of the 2nd Kentucky Infantry. This carte-de-visite view shows Crosthwaite as he appeared in prison at Camp Douglas, Illinois, after his capture at Chickamauga. He was later exchanged and returned to the ranks to serve in the final campaign of the Orphan Brigade in Georgia and South Carolina. (Kentucky Library and Museum, Western Kentucky University.)

Richard L. Usrey from Graves County was elected 2nd lieutenant of Company D, 2nd Kentucky Infantry in July 1861. During skirmish actions along the Kennesaw Line in north Georgia in June 1864, Lieutenant Usrey was severely wounded in the hip and was sent to the hospital. Despite his injury, he recovered sufficiently to return to his company and take part in the final campaign of the war. (Orphan Brigade Kinfolk.)

Born near Frankfort in 1840, Richard Kidder Woodson enlisted in July 1861 in the "Salt River Tigers," Company C, 2nd Kentucky Infantry. During the charge of the Orphan Brigade against massed Federal cannons at Murfreesboro, Tennessee, on January 2, 1863, he was mortally wounded while carrying his regiment's battle flag. For his courage, he was nominated to the Confederate Roll of Honor. (*Confederate Veteran Association*, 1895.)

Roger Weightman Hanson was born in Winchester in 1827 and became colonel of the 2nd Kentucky Infantry in 1861. Hanson led his regiment at Fort Donelson and was promoted to brigadier general in December 1862. He was mortally wounded leading the Orphan Brigade at Murfreesboro and died on January 4, 1863. Hanson is buried in the Lexington Cemetery beneath a monument erected by the veterans of the Orphan Brigade. (Library of Congress.)

A native of Bath County, James M. Bourne was in Alabama when the war started, so he volunteered there. He served in Alabama units until he was transferred to the 5th Kentucky Infantry, Company C, in 1864. Although he had lost an eye to an accidental bayonet wound early in the war, he continued to serve and eventually rose to the rank of sergeant. (Kentucky Historical Society.)

George Bibb Crittenden was born in Russellville on March 20, 1812. He graduated from West Point and served in the Mexican War before becoming a Confederate general in 1861. He commanded the Southern forces at the defeat at Mill Springs in January 1862 (see page 124). Crittenden died on November 27, 1880, and was buried in the family plot in the Frankfort Cemetery. (Kentucky Library and Museum, Western Kentucky University.)

Christopher C. Tinsley (left) of Barren County volunteered for service in Company A, 4th Kentucky Infantry in August 1861. He transferred to the artillery service in 1862 as a member of Cobb's Kentucky Battery. Tinsley died in a Confederate hospital in Okolona, Mississippi, date unknown, and is buried in the Okolona Confederate Cemetery. (Nola Tinsley Willeford, Kevin Morgan, and Glenn Tinsley.)

Born in Bourbon County in 1823, William Peter Bramblett became captain of the "Flat Rock Grays," Company H, 4th Kentucky Infantry, in September 1861. He was mortally wounded at the head of his company during the charge of the Orphan Brigade at Murfreesboro and died in a Federal field hospital. In 1905, his body was reinterred at the Confederate monument in the Paris cemetery. See page 118. (*Confederate Veteran Association*, 1895.)

25

A native of Scott County, Willis S. Roberts was promoted to major of the 4th Kentucky Infantry in December 1862. He was killed during the tragic charge of the Orphan Brigade at Murfreesboro. In this image taken while he was a captain, Roberts is wearing his regulation officer's frock coat with a sword that might have been a model made by Confederate manufacturers L. Haiman and Brother of Columbus, Georgia. (Geoff Walden.)

Pvt. John R. Boyette of Versailles joined Company E of the 4th Kentucky Infantry in October 1861. He was killed during the battle of Baton Rouge on August 5, 1862. In this tintype image, Boyette appears to be wearing civilian clothes, which was the most common Confederate "uniform" early in the war. (Special Collections, University of Kentucky.)

A native of Columbia, Kentucky, George Hector Burton enlisted in Company F, 4th Kentucky Infantry and rose through the ranks to lieutenant. During the Atlanta Campaign of 1864, he was placed in command of the Orphan Brigade sharpshooters. Burton moved to Georgia after the war and became a successful minister in Georgia and South Carolina. Despondent over his failing health, he committed suicide on February 2, 1922. (Geoff Walden.)

John Henry Weller was born in Hardin County on April 11, 1842. He joined the 4th Kentucky Infantry and rose to the rank of captain of Company D, later serving as acting lieutenant colonel. Weller was active in veteran affairs after the war and served on the Chickamauga battlefield commission. He died on October 3, 1912, and was buried in Cave Hill Cemetery in Louisville. (*History of the Orphan Brigade*, 1898.)

Emmeran Bliemel was born in Germany in 1831 and moved to Pennsylvania as a child. He became a priest in 1856 and served in Tennessee units, becoming acting chaplain of the 4th Kentucky Infantry. While ministering to a dying soldier on the battlefield at Jonesboro on August 31, 1864, Bliemel was decapitated by a cannonball. He was the first American Catholic chaplain killed in action. (Saint Vincent Archabbey Archives, Latrobe, Pennsylvania.)

Gen. Benjamin Hardin Helm served in the Kentucky State Guard and raised a cavalry regiment for Confederate service. In 1863, he was placed in command of the Orphan Brigade. Helm was mortally wounded at Chickamauga on September 20, 1863. Upon hearing the outcome of the battle as he lay dying, his final word was "Victory!" In 1884, Helm's body was brought back to Kentucky, where it now rests in the family graveyard in Elizabethtown. (*Sketches of Camp Boone*, 1860.)

Born in Frankfort in 1812, Humphrey Marshall graduated from West Point and commanded volunteers in the Mexican War. He became a Confederate general in 1861, serving in Virginia and Kentucky. He resigned his commission in 1863 and entered the Confederate Congress. Marshall practiced law after the war until his death on March 28, 1872. He is buried in the State Cemetery in Frankfort. (Special Collections, University of Kentucky.)

William Tyler Barry South was born in Breathitt County on November 10, 1842. He commanded Company B, 5th Kentucky Infantry, throughout the war and fought in eastern Kentucky, at Chickamauga, and in the Atlanta Campaign. South had six brothers and three brothers-in-law in Confederate service. He died on November 24, 1932, and was buried in the State Cemetery in Frankfort. (Abbie Wood and Orphan Brigade Kinfolk.)

A native of Johnson County, Martin P. Bailey was a Mexican War veteran who joined Company B, 5th Kentucky Infantry, on September 11, 1862, at Jackson, Kentucky. He was promoted up through the ranks to corporal but was reported as a deserter in November 1863. Bailey died of malaria on October 18, 1870, and was buried in the Bailey Cemetery in Lee County. (Orphan Brigade Kinfolk.)

Nicholas Bartlett Pearce was born in 1828 in Caldwell County. He graduated from West Point and served in the Indian Territory. During the War Between the States, he commanded a brigade of Arkansas militia, assisting in the defeat of the Federal forces at Wilson's Creek. Pearce then served in the Confederate Commissary Department until the end of the war. He died in Dallas on March 8, 1894. (Orphan Brigade Kinfolk.)

Joseph Horace Lewis was born in Barren County in 1824. He formed the 6th Kentucky Infantry in 1861 and fought in all of his regiment's battles except Baton Rouge. Lewis was promoted to brigadier general and commanded the Orphan Brigade through the Atlanta Campaign until the final surrender in Georgia in May 1865. He was extremely popular at Orphan Brigade reunions after the war. (Library of Congress.)

Robert Clinton Bryan was born in Simpson County in 1841 or 1842. He enlisted in June 1862 in the "Buckner Grays," Company I, 6th Kentucky Infantry and fought in all the battles of his company. Bryan died of disease at LaGrange, Georgia, on March 16, 1864, and is buried in the Confederate cemetery there. This early war image shows him armed with a smoothbore musket. (Octagon Hall Museum.)

An illustrious citizen of Hardin County, Martin Hardin Cofer raised a battalion for Confederate service and became lieutenant colonel of the 6th Kentucky Infantry. He was severely wounded at Shiloh and was promoted to colonel of his regiment after Chickamauga, and he later served as provost marshal of the Army of Tennessee. Cofer died on May 22, 1881, and was buried in Elizabethtown. (Joey Oller.)

Luke Kennady was a native of Hardin County who served in Company H of the 6th Kentucky Infantry. He was appointed quartermaster sergeant of his regiment and fought at Shiloh, Chickamauga, and Jonesboro, where he received an arm wound so disabling that it prevented him from further service. He died on March 25, 1898, and was buried in Red Hill Cemetery in Hodgenville. (Kentucky Historical Society.)

Cyrus Wayne Branham was born in Hardin County on July 21, 1838. He joined Company B, 6th Kentucky Infantry and was promoted to corporal in September 1863. He fought in all of his regiment's battles, including the battle of Jonesboro, which ended the Atlanta Campaign of 1864. Branham was killed during his regiment's charge against enemy breastworks at Jonesboro on August 31, 1864. (Horace Clinton Branham III.)

Cyrus Branham was first buried on the battlefield at Jonesboro, but his father traveled to Georgia by wagon in 1865 to retrieve his body for burial in the family cemetery in Vine Grove, Kentucky. Along with Cyrus's remains, his father brought back his original wooden grave marker, which can be seen today in the Hardin County History Museum in Elizabethtown. (Francis Mulquin.)

A native of Barren County, George R. Peden served as a private in the ranks of Company D, 6th Kentucky Infantry. He enlisted at Cave City in November 1861 and fought at Shiloh in April 1862. He died of an undisclosed cause during the service in 1864. In this image, probably taken in 1861, he is wearing a dark woolen frock coat with infantry kepi. (Barren County Clerk.)

John Clifton Peden served with his brother George in Company D of the 6th Kentucky Infantry. Like his brother, he fought at Shiloh in April 1862, then died in 1863 of an unspecified disease. He posed for this picture in his uniform coat, which is a slightly different pattern from his brother's, with an unknown insignia appearing on the collar. (Barren County Clerk.)

A native of Anderson County, George Wilson Humes joined Company G, 6th Kentucky Infantry and fought at Baton Rouge, Jackson, and Chickamauga. When his regiment was converted to mounted infantry in 1864, he served sometimes on horseback and sometimes with the dismounted detachment in the final campaign in South Carolina. In this image, he is seen wearing a "Columbus Depot" jacket. (Richard Quire, Humes's great-great-great grandson.)

Thomas Hercules Hays was born in Hardin County on October 6, 1837. He served in the Kentucky State Guard and was commissioned major of the 6th Kentucky Infantry in October 1861. He later served on several general staffs and ended his service in Savannah. After the war, he engaged in farming, industry, and politics. Hays died in 1909 and is buried in Louisville. (Joseph Hays Rich, Hays's great-great grandson.)

Joseph Tulley Winlock was born in Barren County in 1845. He joined the 6th Kentucky Infantry and fought at Shiloh, Murfreesboro, and in the Atlanta Campaign before being captured during the battle of Atlanta (called Intrenchment Creek by the Orphan Brigade). He died on November 29, 1912, and is buried in the Hiseville Cemetery. This ambrotype shows him wearing a battle shirt, a favorite of Confederates early in the war. (Orphan Brigade Kinfolk.)

Holman Hardin Smith enlisted in Company D, 6th Kentucky Infantry, fought at Baton Rouge, Murfreesboro, and the Atlanta Campaign, and rose to the rank of corporal. In this image, taken in Atlanta in 1864, he is wearing the type of jacket known today as a "Columbus Depot" jacket. Smith died on May 18, 1923, and was buried in Summersville. See page 105. (Sallie Bryan and Tiffany Luchetta, Smith's great-great-great niece.)

The "Kentucky Battle Song" was written in 1861 by Charles Ward, chief musician of the 4th Kentucky Infantry. This song was popular in the Orphan Brigade recruiting camps that were established just across the state line in Tennessee because it celebrated the soldiers' desires to return to Kentucky and turn it into a Confederate state. The song sheet seen here was published in 1864 by Blanton Duncan, who had served as the first colonel of the 1st Kentucky Infantry. The cover of the song sheet shows several depictions of battle flags for the various regiments of the 1st Kentucky "Orphan" Brigade, complete with battle honors and the names of Orphan Brigade unit commanders. Although none of these are true depictions of any surviving Orphan Brigade flag, the illustrations were meant to depict the types of flags under which the unit served. In this case, the dark blue flag with a white disc was designed by Gen. Simon B. Buckner and is best known as the flag of General Hardee's corps. (Steve Menefee.)

One of the most popular soldiers of the Orphan Brigade, Maj. Rice E. Graves commanded a Kentucky battery and served as chief of artillery on General Breckinridge's staff. When Graves was mortally wounded at Chickamauga on September 20, 1863, Breckinridge reported, "a truer friend, a purer patriot, a better soldier never lived." Graves was buried in the Citizens Cemetery in Ringgold, Georgia. (Lee Rowland, Graves's great-great nephew.)

Henry Cornelius Burnett was a colorful member of Kentucky's delegation to the Confederate government. He presided over the secession convention that formed the Provisional Government of Kentucky in November 1861 then was elected colonel of the 8th Kentucky Infantry. Burnett was a strong supporter of Confederate president Jefferson Davis and was one of the most active and vocal members of the "Kentucky bloc" in the Confederate Congress. (Gary Gardner.)

Hugh Henry was born October 30, 1841, in Bourbon County. He rose through the officer ranks in Company H, 4th Kentucky Infantry to command the company in January 1863. Henry fought in every battle of his company, from Shiloh in 1862 to the final battle as mounted infantry in April 1865. He died in 1919 at the Kentucky Confederate Home and was buried in Cave Hill Cemetery in Louisville. (Sam Flora.)

Andrew Jackson Beale was a physician in Cynthiana, Kentucky, who was elected 2nd lieutenant of Company D, 9th Kentucky Infantry. Beale was promoted to captain and appointed as a surgeon in October 1863; he served the remainder of the war in the medical department. After the war he entered local politics then moved to Oklahoma, where he was elected the first mayor of Oklahoma City. (Special Collections, University of Kentucky.)

A native of Russellville, John William Caldwell raised Company A, 9th Kentucky Infantry and rose to the rank of colonel in 1863. He fought in every battle of his regiment, several times serving as acting commander of the Orphan Brigade. After the war Caldwell practiced law and became a Logan County judge, dying on July 4, 1903. In this photograph he posed with his son Barclay. (Joey Oller.)

Pvt. Daniel W. Jenkins joined the Confederate service from Bullitt County, enlisting in Company B, 9th Kentucky Infantry in October 1861. He was killed in action at the battle of Shiloh, Tennessee, during the Orphan Brigade's attacks against the Federal forces on April 6, 1862. Some time in the winter of 1861, probably at Bowling Green, Private Jenkins posed for this image wearing an overcoat. (Stanley Allen Hutson.)

Brothers John Lewis Dunn and Eli Edward Dunn went to war together in Company A, 9th Kentucky Infantry. Cpl. John Dunn was named to the Confederate Roll of Honor for his meritorious service at the battle of Chickamauga, where he was killed in action. In this image, he appears with a U.S. flintlock musket converted to percussion and a pistol stuck in his waist belt. (Marilyn Dunn Carothers.)

Cpl. Eli Edward Dunn was the second of the Dunn brothers to fall in battle. The brothers enlisted in Russellville in September 1861 and served together in the battles of Shiloh, Baton Rouge, Murfreesboro, and Chickamauga. Eli rose to the rank of 1st corporal of his company before being killed in action at Jonesboro, Georgia, during the Atlanta Campaign of 1864. (Marilyn Dunn Carothers.)

Ben Desha, a native of Cynthiana, was elected captain of Company D, 9th Kentucky Infantry in 1861 and was promoted to major in April 1863. He was severely wounded at Shiloh but returned to serve at Jonesboro in August 1864, where he was again severely wounded and was disabled for the rest of the war. Desha died at his home in Cynthiana in 1885. (*Confederate Veteran Association*, 1895.)

The young soldier in this image is thought to be Charles B. Mitchell, a private in Company C, 9th Kentucky Infantry. Many soldiers liked to pose for their first photograph with a couple of pistols that were usually supplied by the photographer. Mitchell also held what was probably a pocket bible in his hand for this image. (William Dunniway and Sam Young.)

S. Abijah Brooks of Bourbon County joined the "Hamilton Guards," Company G, 2nd Kentucky Infantry, in July 1861. He went on to serve in the ranks at Fort Donelson, Hartsville, and Murfreesboro, Tennessee. He was mortally wounded during his regiment's charge at Murfreesboro on January 2, 1863, and died a few days later. (Blue Grass Trust for Historic Preservation.)

Lafayette Bills of Bourbon County was appointed corporal of Company G, 2nd Kentucky Infantry. Company G, known as the Hamilton Guards, fought at Fort Donelson in February 1862 and surrendered when the fort fell. A series of ambrotype images were made of the company's members while they were in prison showing their matching double-breasted frock coats and dark caps with letters "HG." (Blue Grass Trust for Historic Preservation.)

William Preston was born near Louisville in 1816. He served in the Mexican War and in state and national legislatures. He became a Confederate general in April 1862 and commanded units at Corinth, Murfreesboro, and Chickamauga. In 1864, he was transferred to the Trans-Mississippi Department. Preston died on September 21, 1887, and was buried in Cave Hill Cemetery in Louisville. (Special Collections, University of Kentucky.)

Klauber,   Louisville.
882 Fourth Ave.

A native of Frankfort, Thomas Hart Taylor helped raise the 1st Kentucky Infantry in 1861 and was promoted to general in November 1862. He commanded troops in Tennessee, Mississippi, Louisiana, and Alabama. After the war, he served as the chief of police in Louisville for several years. Taylor died on April 12, 1901, and was buried in the State Cemetery in Frankfort. (Library of Congress.)

A native of Todd County, Edward Barker Ross was commissioned captain of Company K, 3rd Kentucky Infantry. In the summer of 1862 at Vicksburg, Ross volunteered to serve onboard the Confederate ironclad CSS *Arkansas*. He was captured and later exchanged in March 1865, after which he continued to serve until his unit surrendered two months later. Ross died at his home on December 7, 1911. (Orphan Brigade Kinfolk.)

John Williams Green enlisted in Company B, 9th Kentucky Infantry and rose to be sergeant major of the regiment. He fought in several battles and was severely wounded at Shiloh. Green returned to Louisville after the war and wrote his memoirs, which were published in 1956 as *Johnny Green of the Orphan Brigade*. He died in 1920 and was buried in Cave Hill Cemetery. (MOLLUS Collection, U.S. Army Military History Institute.)

John Reed joined the Confederate service from Bath County and enlisted in Company C of the 5th Kentucky Infantry. He fought at Chickamauga, Missionary Ridge, and at the first battles of the Atlanta Campaign. He was killed in action at Resaca, Georgia, on May 14, 1864, and is likely buried in one of the graves marked as unknown in the Resaca Confederate Cemetery. (Charles Ketchum.)

John Lewis Rogers was born in 1847. He enlisted in Company E, 6th Kentucky Infantry, serving under Joseph Lewis and Martin Cofer in memorable battles such as Shiloh, Murfreesboro, Chickamauga, and the Atlanta Campaign. The regiment ended its service on May 6, 1865, in Washington, Georgia. After the war, Rogers lived in Franklin, where he died in 1936. See page 109. (Octagon Hall Museum.)

Alexander Humphreys Todd was born into the illustrious Todd family of Lexington in 1839. He was a half-brother of Mary Todd Lincoln. He served as a lieutenant on the staff of his brother-in-law Gen. Ben Hardin Helm, commander of the Orphan Brigade. Todd was killed during an accidental exchange of fire at Baton Rouge, on August 5, 1862, and was later buried in the Todd plot of the Lexington Cemetery. (Joey Oller.)

William Preston was a Mexican War veteran and politician who became a Confederate general. In the summer of 1862, he commanded one of the brigades that contained Kentucky regiments in Mississippi. He was appointed Confederate minister to the Imperial Mexican government in 1864, but he was unable to reach Emperor Maximilian. This carte-de-visite image is marked Havana, Cuba, on the reverse. (Special Collections, University of Kentucky.)

John Cabell Breckinridge of Lexington had an illustrious career in the Confederacy. First leading the Kentucky troops in Tennessee, he rose to the rank of major general and commanded Confederate forces in the Shenandoah Valley in 1864, then was appointed as Confederate secretary of war in February 1865. This painting by E. F. Andrews shows Breckinridge posing in full uniform in his war office. (Kentucky Library and Museum, Western Kentucky University.)

The strain of war is evident on Gen. John C. Breckinridge's face in this photograph taken late in the war or shortly following the end of the war. As a former U.S. vice president, he was forced to flee the country in May 1865 to avoid imprisonment. He returned home in 1869 and was one of the most popular men in the commonwealth until his death in 1875. (Gary Gardner.)

Three

KENTUCKY CONFEDERATE CAVALRY SOLDIERS

John Hunt Morgan of Lexington became one of the most celebrated cavalry commanders of the Civil War. After serving in the Kentucky State Guard, he raised a regiment for Confederate service and fought at Shiloh. In the summer of 1862, Morgan was given an independent command organized of partisan rangers who operated mainly behind enemy lines. Morgan's men burned railroad bridges and military depots in an effort to disrupt the supply of Union forces in Kentucky and Tennessee. See page 58. (Gary Gardner.)

Basil Wilson Duke was Gen. John Hunt Morgan's most trusted subordinate. He commanded the 2nd Kentucky Cavalry after Morgan. He was captured in Ohio in 1863 and remained a prisoner until 1864 (see page 73). Duke commanded the group that escorted Confederate president Davis in his flight in May 1865. In 1867, he published one of the first books of Confederate reminiscences, *A History of Morgan's Cavalry*. (Special Collections, University of Kentucky.)

Leeland Hathaway of Fayette County was one of the most colorful of Kentucky cavalrymen. He served in Quirk's Scouts and the 8th, 9th, and 14th Kentucky Cavalry Regiments. He was captured during the Ohio Raid in July 1863, and he later returned to service. At the end of the war, Hathaway volunteered to act as bodyguard for Varina Davis, wife of Confederate president Jefferson Davis. (Special Collections, University of Kentucky.)

Richard Curd Morgan, a brother of Gen. John Hunt Morgan, became a volunteer aid to Gen. John C. Breckinridge and served on his staff at Shiloh. He went on to serve under Gen. A. P. Hill in the Army of Northern Virginia before returning to the western theater to join his brother's cavalry command in 1863. See pages 59, 73, and 110. (Special Collections, University of Kentucky.)

Another brother of Gen. John Hunt Morgan, Thomas Hunt Morgan was born in Lexington on May 7, 1844. He enlisted in Company B of the 2nd Kentucky Infantry then transferred to the 2nd Kentucky Cavalry, where he became a lieutenant in Company I. He fought in all the cavalry battles of his regiment until he was killed in action at Lebanon, Kentucky, on July 5, 1863. (Special Collections, University of Kentucky.)

Capt. Ralph Sheldon was the daring commander of Company C, 2nd Kentucky Cavalry. He was one of the officers who escaped from prison with Gen. John Hunt Morgan following the Ohio Raid of 1863. Sheldon was recaptured and sent to Fort Delaware, where this carte-de-visite image was taken on July 30, 1864. Sheldon died at his home in Nelson County on March 8, 1895. (Special Collections, University of Kentucky.)

James M. Barlow joined Company C, 9th Kentucky Cavalry in July 1862. He died in Newnan, Georgia, on January 16, 1864, and is buried in the Confederate Cemetery in Marietta. In this image he is armed with two Colt revolvers and a Remington revolver. What appears to be a handkerchief is actually a miniature Confederate First National flag pinned to his jacket. (Kentucky Historical Society.)

Richard R. Worsham was born in Lexington in 1839. He enlisted at Camp Boone, Tennessee, in July 1861, in the 2nd Kentucky Infantry. He escaped capture with his regiment at Fort Donelson and joined the 2nd Kentucky Cavalry, serving in Quirk's Scouts. Worsham was killed in action at the Battle of Lebanon, Kentucky, on July 5, 1863. (*Confederate Veteran Association*, 1895.)

A native of Carroll County, Moses Tandy Pryor entered the Confederate service in October 1862 and became lieutenant colonel of the 4th Kentucky Cavalry under his brother-in-law Col. Henry Giltner. He was captured at Cynthiana, Kentucky, on June 18, 1864, and was held prisoner at Johnson's Island until the close of the war. Pryor moved to Arkansas after the war and died of swamp fever in January 1873. (Orphan Brigade Kinfolk.)

Shelby County natvies William Henry Tucker and John Gill served together in the 8th Kentucky Cavalry. They fought Gen. John Hunt Morgan's cavalry campaigns in Kentucky, before being captured during the Ohio Raid in July 1863. Both were sent to prison at Camp Douglas in Chicago, where this image was made by prison photographer, D.F. Brandon. (Jordan Ricketts and Martha Boltz.)

Pvt. John Parker Jarvis served in Company E, 5th Kentucky Cavalry. He enlisted on September 2, 1862, in Lexington, Kentucky, and fought in Gen. John Hunt Morgan's campaigns in December 1862 and early 1863. He was captured during General Morgan's Ohio Raid in July 1863 and sent to prison at Camp Douglas, where this image was taken. (Morgan's Men Association.)

Capt. Edward T. Rochester served as quartermaster on the staff of the 6th Kentucky Cavalry after joining the regiment in September 1862. He was captured during General Morgan's Ohio Raid in July 1863. In this image, he appears to be wearing a mourning band, a band of cloth worn around the left arm as a memorial for a departed comrade or family member. (Orphan Brigade Kinfolk.)

A native of Taylor County, Richard Archer Webster was commissioned a lieutenant in Company E, 6th Kentucky Cavalry in September 1862 and was captured during Gen. John Hunt Morgan's Ohio Raid in July 1863. This image of Lieutenant Webster was taken while he was a prisoner at the Allegheny Prison in Pittsburgh. (Kentucky Historical Society.)

This unidentified Confederate officer from Kentcky wears the rank of a Captain, but in an unusual manner. He has turned down the standing collar of his frock coat, and the three bars of his Captain's rank appear on the lapels, with the coat worn open to show his decorated vest. (Orphan Brigade Kinfolk.)

James David Holding enlisted in Company E, 5th Kentucky Cavalry at Lexington on September 2, 1862. While acting as lieutenant of his company, he was captured at Buffington Island on July 19, 1863, during Gen. John Hunt Morgan's Ohio Raid. He escaped from Camp Douglas in December 1863. Holding died on March 7, 1930, and was buried in the Georgetown Cemetery. (Kittie and Bill Dupps.)

C. C. Corbett commanded an artillery battery that was popularly known as "Morgan's Bull Pups." Armed with highly mobile 12-pounder mountain howitzers, Corbett's battery did good service alongside the 2nd Kentucky Cavalry in Gen. John Hunt Morgan's campaigns. In this photograph taken while Corbett was a prisoner, he wears a style of cavalry jacket favored by Morgan's men and a two-piece "CS" buckle. (Kentucky Library and Museum, Western Kentucky University.)

A native of Lincoln County, Lt. William Porter Crow served in Company B, 6th Kentucky Cavalry and was captured in July 1863. He was one of the famous "Immortal 600," a group of Confederate prisoners who were forced to endure harsh conditions under friendly fire at Morris Island. Crow died on November 12, 1865, and was buried in Stanford. He was a victim of lung disease resulting from his wartime imprisonment. (Morgan's Men Association.)

This photograph shows Gen. John Hunt Morgan as he appeared at the height of his success as a Confederate cavalry leader in 1863. Morgan specialized in classic guerrilla warfare behind enemy lines and excelled as an independent commander by keeping enemy leaders guessing where he would turn up next to burn supply depots and interrupt lines of communication. See pages 49 and 93. (Special Collections, University of Kentucky.)

John Hunt Morgan married his second wife, Martha "Mattie" Ready, on December 14, 1862, just after his promotion to brigadier general. Shortly after the wedding, Morgan left on his famous Christmas Raid, followed by the Ohio Raid in 1863. Upon his death in September 1864, Mattie went into mourning and devoted herself to raising their daughter Johnnie, who was born after the general's death. (Library of Congress.)

Col. Richard "Dick" Morgan, a brother of Gen. John Hunt Morgan, was captured with his brother during the Ohio Raid in July 1863 and remained a prisoner of war until being exchanged in August 1864. He returned to his home in Lexington after the war and engaged in the manufacturing of hemp rope before his death in 1918. See pages 51, 73, and 110. (Special Collections, University of Kentucky.)

Francis Key Morgan, the youngest brother of Gen. John Hunt Morgan, was born in Lexington on August 23, 1845. He enlisted in the 2nd Kentucky Cavalry in 1862, when he was 17. Fighting in various cavalry actions, he surrendered in Augusta, Georgia, in May 1865. Morgan was a businessman in Lexington after the war and died at his home on October 6, 1878. (*Confederate Veteran Association*, 1895.)

Lt. James L. West joined Company A, 2nd Kentucky Cavalry and was one of the first officers to volunteer for service under John Hunt Morgan. He served as a staff officer for Colonel Morgan and was killed in action during the battle of Shiloh on April 6, 1862, while charging with Morgan against the Federal forces in a patch of woods on the western side of the battlefield. (Orphan Brigade Kinfolk.)

James Wintersmith served as an orderly for Gen. John Hunt Morgan and was wounded at Hartsville, Tennessee, on December 7, 1862. Called the "pets of Morgan's Cavalry," the youthful orderlies such as Jimmie Wintersmith proved their worth in battle by carrying dispatches in the thick of the fight. After the war, Wintersmith served as sergeant at arms in the U.S. House of Representatives. (*Battles and Sketches of the Army of Tennessee*, 1906.)

Alfred W. Stanhope served as a sergeant in Company A of the 2nd Kentucky Cavalry. He was wounded in an action at Bacon Creek, Kentucky, during Gen. John Hunt Morgan's Christmas Raid in December 1862 and was captured at Buffington Island, Ohio, during Morgan's Great Raid in July 1863. He was sent to prison at Camp Morton and later to Camp Douglas, where this image was made. (Karl E. Sundstrom.)

Joseph B. Stanhope served with his brother Alfred in Company A, 2nd Kentucky Cavalry. Along with his brother and most of the other members of his regiment, Stanhope was captured at Buffington Island, Ohio, and sent as a prisoner of war to Camp Morton and Camp Douglas. He was exchanged along with his brother Alfred at the end of the war in May 1865. (Karl E. Sundstrom.)

Thomas B. Webber was made major of the 2nd Kentucky Cavalry in January 1863. One of Gen. John Hunt Morgan's best field commanders, he was captured during the Ohio Raid in July 1863 and sent to the Ohio State Penitentiary with Morgan. He was paroled in August 1864 and returned to serve under Gen. Basil Duke. (Orphan Brigade Kinfolk.)

John William Hite was born in Logan County on April 19, 1846. He enlisted in Company B, 2nd Kentucky Cavalry and was captured along with most of his regiment at Buffington Island, Ohio, on July 19, 1863. This image was taken while he was a prisoner of war at Camp Douglas. Hite died on January 9, 1916, and was buried in McCracken County. (Orphan Brigade Kinfolk.)

Belford Duke Smith was born on October 31, 1845, in Todd County, Kentucky. He enlisted in Company B of the 2nd Kentucky Cavalry in 1862 and was captured during the Ohio Raid in the summer of 1863. Smith was paroled at the end of the war and returned home to his farm. He died on June 22, 1901, in Montgomery County, Tennessee. (Orphan Brigade Kinfolk.)

Capt. William E. Curry volunteered for Confederate service in Clark County in September 1862 and was appointed assistant quartermaster of the 8th Kentucky Cavalry. Captured during Morgan's Ohio Raid in July 1863, he remained a prisoner for the remainder of the war. He returned to Kentucky after his release in 1865, dying at his home in 1883. See page 87. (Kentucky Library and Museum, Western Kentucky University.)

Adam Rankin Johnson was born on February 8, 1834, in Henderson, Kentucky. He led the 10th Kentucky Partisan Rangers in cavalry actions behind enemy lines, being promoted to general on June 1, 1864. Johnson was blinded by accidental friendly fire in August 1864. He was a prominent citizen of Texas after the war, dying in 1922. (Mike Sisk.)

These officers of Adam Johnson's 10th Kentucky Partisan Rangers and other units posed for a group image. The regiment operated mostly behind enemy lines and also served under Gen. John Hunt Morgan. The three standing at left are, from the left, Capt. John H. Hamby of Company K, Capt. Henry Clay Meriwether of Company I, and Lt. Jack Allen of Company L. Reclining in the center of the image is Capt. Samuel Burk Taylor of Company E. (Mike Sisk.)

Born in 1845, Hiram C. Rogers joined Company C of the 9th Kentucky Cavalry in September 1862 in Lexington, Kentucky, and was later transferred to the 2nd Kentucky Cavalry. He served in the cavalry campaigns under Gen. John Hunt Morgan, including the Christmas Raid of 1862 and the Ohio Raid of 1863. (Special Collections, University of Kentucky.)

A native of Jefferson County, John Andrew Broaddus enlisted in Company I, 2nd Kentucky Cavalry in September 1862. He fought in the cavalry actions under Gen. John Hunt Morgan at Elizabethtown, Lebanon, Green River Bridge, and in the Ohio Raid in July 1863. After the war, he returned to his home and was buried in Cave Hill Cemetery in Louisville. (Joey Oller and Orphan Brigade Kinfolk.)

Born in Fayette County on April 16, 1842, Lt. Waller O. Bullock served as an adjutant for Col. Adam R. Johnson of the 10th Kentucky Partisan Rangers (see page 64). He was captured at Grubbs Crossroads, Kentucky, in August 1864 but was released soon afterwards when his grandmother bribed his captors with gold. He later served as aide-de-camp to Gen. George B. Hodge. (Orphan Brigade Kinfolk.)

Mike C. Saufley joined Roberts' Kentucky Cavalry Company at Livingston, Tennessee, on January 24, 1862, just after the company had fought at Mill Springs (see page 124). Roberts' unit became Company H of the 6th Kentucky Cavalry, and Saufley was elected lieutenant. He was captured during Gen. John Hunt Morgan's Ohio Raid in July 1863 and was sent to Allegheny Prison in Pittsburgh, where this image was taken. (Morgan's Men Association.)

Capt. Robert D. Logan commanded Company A of the 6th Kentucky Cavalry. He was captured during General Morgan's Ohio Raid in 1863 and was one of the famous "Immortal 600," a group of Confederate prisoners who were forced to endure harsh conditions under friendly fire at Charleston. Logan survived this treatment and the war. He died in Boyle County on June 25, 1896. See page 123. (Orphan Brigade Kinfolk.)

Matthew D. Logan of Lancaster, Kentucky, was a graduate of the Jefferson Medical College in Philadelphia but he abandoned his civilian medical practice to raise a company for Confederate service. Capt. Logan's Company I, 3rd/7th Kentucky Cavalry served under Gen. John Hunt Morgan. His brothers Robert and Alison served in the 6th Kentucky Cavalry. Logan died on June 18, 1898. (Orphan Brigade Kinfolk.)

A native of White Sulphur in Caldwell County, Alexander Thomas joined the 5th Kentucky Cavalry in March 1863 with the rank of captain. He served on the regimental staff as assistant chief of staff. He was captured during Gen. John Hunt Morgan's Ohio Raid in July 1863 and was sent to prison at Fort Delaware. Thomas apparently borrowed a major's coat when he posed for this image. (Kentucky Historical Society.)

E. W. McLean served as captain of Company B, 2nd Kentucky Cavalry. He led his company in General Morgan's Christmas Raid into Kentucky in December 1862, when Morgan's forces burned two large railroad trestles that were key to supplying the Federal army in Tennessee. He was captured during the Ohio Raid in July 1863 and was sent to prison at Fort Delaware, where this image was made. (Orphan Brigade Kinfolk.)

Family records identify this soldier as Pvt. Merritt Calvin Alloway of Company D, 1st Kentucky Cavalry. Alloway was born in Bullitt County on February 23, 1837. He fought at Chickamauga and in the Atlanta Campaign, and in May 1865, he was part of the escort for Pres. Jefferson Davis. It is not clear why this photograph shows him wearing the uniform of a Confederate captain. (Jordan Ricketts.)

Born in 1838, William Harvey Edwards enlisted in Woodford County on September 2, 1862. He joined Company D of the 5th Kentucky Cavalry and served as a private. The 5th Kentucky Cavalry, under Col. D. Howard Smith, fought in cavalry actions under Gen. John Hunt Morgan in 1862 and 1863. Edwards died on March 2, 1905. (Special Collections, University of Kentucky.)

This image shows one of the Rogers brothers of Lexington, most likely Capt. James Thomas Rogers of Company D, 13th Kentucky Cavalry. This regiment, commanded by Col. Ben Caudill, was also known as the 10th Kentucky Mounted Rifles and 11th Kentucky Mounted Infantry. Rogers, who had been born in 1841, took command of the company in April 1864. (Special Collections, University of Kentucky.)

Born in Lexington in 1848, Hugh William Rogers served in Company D, 13th Kentucky Cavalry under the command of his brother James. Their brother Hiram served in the 9th Kentucky Cavalry (see page 65). Hugh Rogers was wounded and captured in 1864 and remained a prisoner for the rest of the war. He died on November 11, 1891, and was buried in Paris, Kentucky. (Special Collections, University of Kentucky.)

George Washington Hunter was born in Nelson County in 1834. He joined Company G of the 8th Kentucky Cavalry in September 1862 and served as a 2nd lieutenant under the command of his brother John. He was captured during the Ohio Raid in July 1863 and sent to the Allegheny Prison in Pittsburgh, where this image was taken. Hunter died in Louisville on December 30, 1920. (Morgan's Men Association.)

John D. Fields was born on April 19, 1845, and served in the 2nd Kentucky Cavalry and Quirk's Scouts under Gen. John Hunt Morgan. He escaped capture on the Ohio Raid of 1863 and joined the command of Gen. John S. Williams in southwest Virginia. He later served under Gen. Adam Johnson and was then appointed lieutenant in Company B, 14th Kentucky Cavalry. (Mike Sisk.)

71

Elmore D. Warder commanded Company K, 7th Kentucky Cavalry and was captured during Gen. Morgan's Ohio Raid in July 1863. Warder died while a prisoner at Fort Delaware on August 11, 1864. He was photographed wearing the regulation rank of three collar bars for a captain, along with unusual shoulder boards, which resemble the shoulder boards worn by officers of the Kentucky State Guard in 1860. (Kentucky Historical Society.)

Benjamin Dominic Edward Cambron was born in Marion County on September 19, 1841. He served as a private in Company K, 8th Kentucky Cavalry and was captured near Cheshire, Ohio, in July 1863. He was sent as a prisoner to Camp Douglas in Illinois, where this image was taken. Cambron died on April 20, 1921, and was buried in the St. Rose Cemetery in Springfield. (Frank Walker.)

A group of Confederate officers, mostly from General Morgan's command, poses at Fort Delaware prison in May 1864. From left to right are (first row) Col. Joseph T. Tucker, Capt. Hart Gibson, Brig. Gen. Robert B. Vance, Rev. Isaac W. K. Handy, Bailey B. Key (in front), Gen. M. Jeff Thompson, and Col. William W. Ward; (second row) Lt. N. H. Brogden, Lt. H. H. Smith, Lt. Joseph J. Andrews, Lt. Col. Cicero Coleman, Col. Richard Curd Morgan, Lt. Charlton H. Morgan, Col. Basil Duke, and Lt. John A. Tomlinson. (Special Collections, University of Kentucky.)

This Kentucky cavalry soldier has been identified as Presley Smith. He wears cavalry boots and a jacket with an unusual cuff and collar trim. His belt is fastened with two small roller buckles, which was a common style of civilian-type waist belts. He is armed with two revolvers in belt holsters, which appear to have tie-down strings hanging down each leg. (Kentucky Library and Museum, Western Kentucky University.)

These three unidentified Kentucky cavalrymen were probably members of the Smith family. They likely served in units under Gen. John Hunt Morgan's command. Each is armed with multiple Colt revolvers, the two seated troopers holding Colt Model 1860 Army pistols in .44 caliber. The standing soldier is wearing an oval brass CS belt plate, modeled after the regulation US belt plate. (Kentucky Library and Museum, Western Kentucky University.)

This cavalry soldier appears in the group photograph on page 74. He posed for this seated image wearing a black plumed slouch hat, pinned up on the side, which was a favorite style of cavalrymen. He still holds his Colt Army revolver, but he has changed his belt for a regulation U.S. sword belt with an eagle belt plate. (Kentucky Library and Museum, Western Kentucky University.)

Like many cavalrymen, this soldier from the group image on page 74 preferred to carry multiple pistols, since the cap-and-ball revolvers of the period were difficult to reload, particularly from horseback. With these five pistols, the soldier had 30 shots ready to fire before he needed to reload. Morgan's cavalry operated almost exclusively with revolvers and carbines instead of swords. (Kentucky Library and Museum, Western Kentucky University.)

75

A native of Bourbon County, Joseph Keesee served as a lieutenant in Company D, 8th Kentucky Cavalry. He fought in several Kentucky battles including Cumberland Gap, Danville, Morgan's Christmas Raid, and battles in 1863 such as Green River Bridge and Lebanon. He was captured during the Ohio Raid in July 1863 and was sent to Camp Douglas prison, where he died of disease on November 14, 1863. (*Confederate Veteran Association*, 1895.)

George Will Jackson was born in Fleming County on May 20, 1835, and became captain of Company B, 2nd Battalion Kentucky Mounted Rifles. He was captured at Cynthiana in June 1864 and was imprisoned on Johnson's Island, Ohio. Jackson made a daring escape over frozen Lake Erie but was recaptured and remained a prisoner for the rest of the war. Jackson passed away on February 19, 1909. (Orphan Brigade Kinfolk.)

John Stuart Williams was born in 1818 near Mount Sterling, Kentucky. His actions in command of the 4th Kentucky Volunteers in the Mexican War earned him the nickname "Cerro Gordo." He raised the 5th Kentucky Infantry in 1861, and he later led a colorful career as a general in the Confederate army. He died on July 17, 1898, and was buried in Winchester. (Library of Congress.)

Born in Hardin County in 1843, Clinton Augustus Lewis volunteered for Confederate service in the 1st Kentucky Infantry in 1861. When that regiment's enlistment was complete and the unit was disbanded in May 1862, he enlisted in Company C of the 2nd Kentucky Cavalry. Lewis became 2nd corporal of the company on June 2, 1862. Lewis died in Glendale on May 2, 1896. See page 16. (Gary Gardner.)

These troopers of Company B, 2nd Kentucky Cavalry were captured with Gen. John Hunt Morgan's command on the Ohio Raid in July 1863 and were photographed at Camp Douglas prison. From left to right are (first row) Sgt. Jefferson M. Barbee, Pvt. George P. Gillum, Pvt. Thomas W. Mason, and Sgt. Johnson P. West; (second row) H. B. Mason (a civilian) and Sgt. Dean K. Mason. (Karl E. Sundstrom.)

David Waller Chenault was born near Richmond in 1826. In September 1862, he raised the 11th Kentucky Cavalry and became its colonel. Serving under Gen. John Hunt Morgan, he was killed instantly when a musket ball struck him in the head while he was leading a charge at Green River Bridge near Tebbs Bend, Kentucky on July 4, 1863. This image was probably taken in Richmond, Virginia, in January 1863. (*Confederate Veteran Association*, 1895.)

Capt. Bolen (or Bowling) Emory Roberts joined the cavalry from Wayne County in January 1862. He commanded Company H, 6th Kentucky Cavalry, during the Great Raid in July 1863. He was captured at Buffington Island and was imprisoned with General Morgan in the Ohio State Penitentiary. After the war, he wrote an interesting article about the horrendous conditions in prison. (Orphan Brigade Kinfolk.)

A native of Webster County, William Richard Wallace served in Company A, 1st Kentucky Cavalry and in the Signal Corps. Wallace was captured at Jonesboro, Georgia, in 1864 and remained a prisoner until the end of the war. He died in Pine Grove, Arkansas, on January 17, 1927. In this image, Wallace posed with his Colt Navy revolver and a "US" belt buckle worn upside down. (Orphan Brigade Kinfolk.)

Thomas Young Brent Jr. was born on December 29, 1835, in Paris, Kentucky. He joined the Confederate service in September 1862 and became major and later lieutenant colonel of the 5th Kentucky Cavalry, serving under Gen. Abraham Buford and Gen. John Hunt Morgan. He was killed in an attack on a Union position at Green River Bridge near Tebbs Bend, Kentucky, on July 4, 1863. (*Confederate Veteran Association*, 1895.)

Van J. Sellers served as lieutenant of Company A, 2nd Kentucky Cavalry and was transferred to the 9th Tennessee Cavalry. Sellers was captured during Morgan's Ohio Raid and was sent to the Allegheny Penitentiary in Pittsburgh, where this image was taken. Sellers complained in letters home that the prison steam pipes froze in the harsh winter of 1864, and no heat made it to the Confederates' cells. (Morgan's Men Association.)

Dr. William Hays (or Hayes) joined the Confederate army in 1861 and became lieutenant of Company B, 2nd Kentucky Cavalry. Serving under Gen. John Hunt Morgan in 1862–1863, he was captured during the Great Raid in Ohio in July 1863. This photograph was taken while Hays was a prisoner at the Allegheny Prison in Pittsburgh. See page 87. (Kentucky Library, Western Kentucky University.)

Maj. William G. Bullitt was born in Shelby County on March 16, 1833. He raised a company for infantry service then joined the staff of the 6th Kentucky Cavalry. He commanded this regiment during General Morgan's Ohio Raid in 1863 and conducted the gallant rearguard defense at Buffington Island. Along with his unit, he was captured and made a prisoner of war at Fort Delaware. (Orphan Brigade Kinfolk.)

Born in 1844, Alexander W. Macklin joined Company C, 9th Kentucky Cavalry. He was promoted to corporal and served under Gen. Joseph Wheeler during the Atlanta Campaign, where he suffered his only wound when his thumb was shot off at the Battle of Atlanta in July 1864. For this image he posed with a Starr revolver stuck in his belt. See page 110. (Ann Macklin Peel.)

Called one of the handsomest captains in his regiment, Richard O. Gathright commanded Company H of the 4th Kentucky Cavalry after he joined the Confederate service in July 1862. He once narrowly avoided capture by the enemy at Pughs Hill in East Tennessee in October 1863 by walking 16 miles to rejoin his company. Gathright's regiment served mostly in eastern Kentucky, eastern Tennessee, and southwest Virginia. (Orphan Brigade Kinfolk.)

Born in Jefferson County in 1838, Thomas Walker Bullitt joined Company C, 2nd Kentucky Cavalry. He was promoted to lieutenant and was dangerously wounded and captured in 1863. He was a prisoner for the remainder of the war. After returning home, he practiced law in Louisville. Bullitt died on March 3, 1910, and was buried in the Oxmoor Cemetery in Jefferson County. (Lowry Watkins Jr. and Orphan Brigade Kinfolk.)

Edward Darnaby Johnson was born on his family's farm in Fayette County in 1842. He enlisted in Company A of the 8th Kentucky Cavalry in September 1862 and was made a corporal in his company. He was captured during Morgan's Ohio Raid in July 1863 and died of measles on November 19, 1863, while he was a prisoner at Camp Douglas in Chicago. (William Johnson.)

John M. Porter was appointed 2nd lieutenant of Company E, 9th Kentucky Cavalry. In May 1862, he made a daring reconnaissance behind enemy lines with Thomas Henry Hines and others from Gen. John Hunt Morgan's scouts. The information they gathered on the Federal forces and supply lines was quite valuable to Morgan for planning his actions in the summer of 1862. (Kentucky Library and Museum, Western Kentucky University.)

A native of Lancaster, Henry D. Brown served as a lieutenant in Company C, 3rd/7th Kentucky Cavalry. In company with most of the officers of his regiment, he was captured during Gen. John Hunt Morgan's Ohio Raid in July 1863. This photograph was taken while Brown was a prisoner at the Western Penitentiary in Pittsburgh. See page 87. (Kentucky Library and Museum, Western Kentucky University.)

John G. Fible enlisted in Company H, 4th Kentucky Cavalry in 1862 and served under the leadership of Capt. Richard O. Gathright (see page 82). Under the command of Col. Henry Giltner, the 4th Kentucky Cavalry served in eastern Tennessee and southwestern Virginia and was often in units commanded by Gen. John S. Williams. The regiment also served under Gen. John Hunt Morgan in the summer of 1864. (Orphan Brigade Kinfolk.)

Alford Norman Beckner was born on September 21, 1840 or 1845, in Virginia. He joined the Confederate army in September 1862 in Hopkins County and enlisted in Company K, 10th Kentucky Partisan Rangers under Col. Adam R. Johnson. Beckner later served in Capt. John Dortch's 2nd Battalion Kentucky Cavalry. He died in Caldwell County on October 25, 1929. For this image, he posed with a Colt revolver. (Orphan Brigade Kinfolk.)

Searles L. Davis enlisted in "Davis' Rangers," Company H, 1st Kentucky Infantry, in June 1861. He served with this regiment in Northern Virginia, fighting in the Battle of Dranesville on December 20, 1861. When the regiment's enlistment was up, Davis enlisted in the 2nd Kentucky Cavalry. He was captured on General Morgan's Ohio Raid in July 1863, and this image was taken at Camp Douglas prison. (Gary Gardner.)

A native of Allen County, William W. Page was elected lieutenant of Company F, 6th Kentucky Infantry and later joined Quirk's Scouts. This unit was the "eyes and ears" of Gen. John Hunt Morgan's cavalry forces and often ranged far ahead of the main body to gather vital information on the enemy. Page was captured in July 1863, and this image was taken while he was a prisoner. (Morgan's Men Association.)

These officers of Morgan's command posed in the Western Penitentiary in Pittsburgh. From left to right are Capt. William E. Curry, 8th Kentucky Cavalry (see page 63); Lt. Andrew J. Church, 3rd/7th Kentucky Cavalry (see page 89); Lt. Leeland Hathaway, 8th Kentucky Cavalry (see page 50); Lt. Henry D. Brown, 3rd/7th Kentucky Cavalry (see page 84); and Lt. William Hays, 2nd Kentucky Cavalry (see page 81). (Special Collections, University of Kentucky.)

Maj. Nathan Parker joined the 4th Kentucky Cavalry from Trimble County. Known as the "Stonewall" of his regiment, Parker's last words when mortally wounded at Wytheville, Virginia, on May 10, 1864, were, "Charge them, my brave boys!" He was buried on the field, but in 1866 his body was brought to his home in Bedford, Kentucky, for a burial service attended by over 3,000 people. (Orphan Brigade Kinfolk.)

William S. Henry Holloway had an unusual career in the Confederate army. He first enlisted in the 2nd Kentucky Cavalry but changed his name and joined Company K of the 12th Missouri Cavalry, serving with the Confederate guerrilla leader William Quantrill. Family legend says that he claimed to be a Union veteran after the war because he feared the repercussions of having been a guerrilla fighter. (Octagon Hall Museum.)

Capt. Thomas H. Shanks raised Company B of the 6th Kentucky Cavalry in September 1862 at Stanford, Kentucky. He commanded his company during the Battles of Perryville and Murfreesboro and was captured in January 1863 and paroled. He was captured again at Cheshire, Ohio, on July 20, 1863, during General Morgan's Great Raid. (Kentucky Library and Museum, Western Kentucky University.)

These comrades of the 2nd Kentucky Cavalry posed for this group image while they were in prison at Camp Douglas, Illinois. From left to right are (first row) Sgt. Resin R. Simmons, Cpl. Harmon H. Barlow, Pvt. Charles W. Haddox, Pvt. Woodford W. Longmore, and Pvt. William B. Lewis; (second row) Sgt. John W. Friddle, Pvt. S. George Adams, Pvt. Otway B. Norvell, Pvt. Isham Fielding Davis, and Cpl. Thomas W. Bibb. (Scott E. Sallee.)

Andrew J. Church volunteered for service at Lexington, Kentucky, in September 1862, and was made 2nd lieutenant of Company K, 3rd Kentucky Cavalry (this regiment was also known as the 7th Kentucky Cavalry). Church was captured in Ohio in July 1863. He posed for this photograph while he was a prisoner at the Western Penitentiary in Pittsburgh. See page 87. (Kentucky Library and Museum, Western Kentucky University.)

Born in Lexington in 1841, John Breckinridge Castleman served as major of the 2nd Kentucky Cavalry. He later led a band of guerrillas and was captured and sentenced to death but was saved by a personal note from President Lincoln. Castleman commanded, as a general in the U.S. Army, a cavalry unit in the Spanish-American War. He died in 1918 and was buried in Cave Hill Cemetery in Louisville. See pages 98 and 123. (Special Collections, University of Kentucky.)

Humphreys Castleman enlisted as a private in Company D, 2nd Kentucky Cavalry under the command of his brother John. His regiment served in memorable actions such as the Christmas Raid of 1862 into Kentucky and the Great Raid of 1863 through Indiana and Ohio. After the war, Castleman returned to his home in Lexington and was a member of the Breckinridge Camp 100, United Confederate Veterans. (Special Collections, University of Kentucky.)

William Francis Corbin was born in Campbell County in 1833 and served in the 4th Kentucky Cavalry. On a recruiting mission in Kentucky in 1863, he was captured, accused of spying, and sentenced to death. On May 15, 1863, Corbin and a comrade were executed by firing squad at Johnson's Island, Ohio. His body was returned to Kentucky, where it rests in a family cemetery in Campbell County. (*Confederate Veteran Association*, 1895.)

Hylan Benton Lyon recruited and armed an artillery battery from the Eddyville area, which later became famously known as Cobb's Battery of the Orphan Brigade. He was then commissioned as lieutenant colonel of the 8th Kentucky Infantry and served at Fort Donelson and Vicksburg. Lyon was promoted to general in June 1864 and commanded a cavalry brigade under Gen. Nathan Bedford Forrest. He died in 1927 and is buried in Eddyville. (Tom Prince.)

Born in Meade County on February 3, 1838, James A. Shacklett enlisted in the 3rd Tennessee Cavalry but transferred to Company E of the 2nd (Woodward's) Kentucky Cavalry. James returned home to Meade County and married Eleanor Warfield in January 1867. Both are buried in the Buck Grove Cemetery. James died on May 21, 1909. In this image, he posed with a heavy cavalry saber and a Colt's revolver in his belt. (Jean Murray.)

J. L. Egbert enlisted in Company A, 12th Kentucky Cavalry, on April 15, 1864. The 12th Kentucky Cavalry served in a Kentucky brigade under the famous Confederate cavalry leader Nathan Bedford Forrest in battles such as Brice's Crossroads and Union City. However, Egbert was reported as a deserter on May 1, 1864, at McMinnville, Tennessee. (Gary Gardner.)

The weariness of war shows plainly on the face of Gen. John Hunt Morgan in this image taken in 1864. By this time in the war, Morgan was worn out from capture, imprisonment, escape, and the death of his first child. Vowing that the Yankees would never take him prisoner again, Morgan was killed on September 4, 1864, when his command was surprised by Union cavalry. (Special Collections, University of Kentucky.)

Thomas Bronston Collins was born in Madison County on October 4, 1842. He served in Gen. Felix Zollicoffer's forces in the Mill Springs area (see page 124) then became a captain in the 11th Kentucky Cavalry. He fought in Gen. Morgan's Ohio Raid of 1863, where he evaded capture by swimming the Ohio River. He went to Canada and participated in the raid on St. Albans, Vermont, then made his way to Paris, France, where he died in 1869. (*Confederate Veteran Association*, 1895.)

The best-known Confederate guerrilla fighter operating in Kentucky was Marcellus Jerome Clarke, who was known to history as "Sue Mundy." Born in Simpson County in 1844 or 1845, he served in the 4th Kentucky Infantry then in Morgan's Cavalry before becoming a guerrilla leader in 1864. Due to his long hair and youthful looks, a Louisville newspaper editor dubbed him "Sue Mundy." Clarke was captured on March 12, 1865, and hanged in Louisville three days later. He is buried in Franklin. (Octagon Hall Museum.)

Three of the most notorious Kentucky Confederate guerrilla fighters posed for a group picture that was probably taken in late 1864. From left to right are Henry C. Magruder, Marcellus Jerome Clarke "Sue Mundy," and Samuel O. "One-Arm" Berry. All three came to tragic ends. Magruder and Clarke were captured in March 1865, and Clarke was executed without delay, but due to a severe wound, Magruder was not executed until October 20. Berry had lost an arm during a farming accident and turned guerrilla during the war. Berry was captured and spent seven years in a prison in New York before dying of consumption in 1872. (Frank Walker.)

Four

CONFEDERATE VETERANS
MEET AFTER THE WAR

Kentucky Confederate veterans were quick to form associations after the war. Morgan's Men held their first reunion in Lexington in April 1868, on the occasion of General Morgan's reburial there. They continued to meet into the 1920s, along with the veterans of the Orphan Brigade, who held their first reunion in 1882. The Confederate Veteran Association of Kentucky was formed in 1890. This envelope came from the papers of Lt. Col. Cicero Coleman, 8th Kentucky Cavalry. (Geoff Walden.)

Jesse Wilson Durham led a parade in Paris, Kentucky, around 1900. He served in Company E, 6th Kentucky Infantry at Vicksburg, Baton Rouge, Murfreesboro, Chickamauga, and in the final campaign in South Carolina. In 1865, Durham married a girl he had met in South Carolina, and they later moved to Texas, where he died on January 18, 1918. He was buried in Oak Cliff Cemetery in Dallas. (Elaine Whiddon and Orphan Brigade Kinfolk.)

John S. Bell joined the Confederate service from Shepherdsville and fought as a member of Company D, 1st Kentucky Cavalry. He was born in Bullitt County on September 9, 1844, and died in Shepherdsville on February 15, 1915. Bell was buried in the Hebron Cemetery in Shepherdsville. He proudly posed in his Confederate veteran coat that is complete with Orphan Brigade reunion ribbon for this picture. (Orphan Brigade Kinfolk.)

Comrades from Company C, 9th Kentucky Infantry, posed for a group photograph at an Orphan Brigade reunion. The occasion is believed to be the large Confederate veterans reunion in Louisville in June 1905; however, one copy of the photograph is dated September 20, 1906 (the anniversary of the Battle of Chickamauga). From left to right are (first row) Pvt. Ignatius P. Barnard, Pvt. James S. Chinn, 2nd Lt. James W. Ford, Pvt. John L. Taylor, and 1st Sgt. Alexander T. Hines; (second row) 4th Sgt. Stephen W. Rowan, Pvt. William Rumsey Chapman, Pvt. Lycurgus T. Reid, and Pvt. John W. Chinn. These men, all from Ohio County, served together in battles such as Shiloh (where Hines was wounded), Murfreesboro, Chickamauga (where Chapman, James Chinn, Ford, and Taylor were wounded), Missionary Ridge, and the 120 days of the Atlanta Campaign in 1864, where Reid and Rowan were wounded. Reminiscing after the war, Lycurgus Reid said, "I teach my children to honor the men of the Orphan Brigade above all others." (David W. Neal, great-great grandson of "Curg" Reid.)

The smiling veteran in the foreground of this parade is Thompson Hardin Jones, who served in the "Kentucky Minute Men," Company K, 1st Kentucky Infantry. In a letter dated December 12, 1862, he informed his family, "I do not despair of the success of our cause. We *will* gain our independence, and my dear native Kentucky will form one of the brightest stars in the constellation of the Confederacy." (Melissa Jo Goodwin.)

These leaders of the United Confederate Veterans (UCV) in Kentucky formed the executive committee for the 1900 reunion in Louisville. From left to right are (first row) George Gaulbert, Thomas D. Osborne, Bennett H. Young (see page 114), William B. Haldeman, and John B. Castleman (see pages 90 and 123); (second row) John Barbee Pirtle, William M. Marriner, James W. Bowles, John H. Leathers, and Sam H. Buchanan. (Orphan Brigade Kinfolk.)

Veterans of Colonel Chenault's 11th Kentucky Cavalry, Morgan's Men, gathered for a reunion in Danville about 1920. From left to right are (first row) E. P. Halley, N. N. Offutt, J. M. Craig, James N. Parker, Harry W. Piper, Ely Blackburn, John D. Walker, N. B. Deatherage, Joseph S. Buckner, J. B. White, Alex Tribble, Walter Shropshire, Harry Shaw Sr., and W. T. B. South (see page 29); (second row) Ben Stiff, W. C. Stiff, E. P. Thomasson, R. M. Redd, T. D. English, J. A. Yeager, J. M. Conway, J. S. Coke, Charles H. Lee Jr., Beriah Magoffin, W. J. Hanna, and George W. Muir. (Special Collections, University of Kentucky.)

These veterans from Clark County all served in Company C of the 11th Kentucky Cavalry under Col. David W. Chenault (see page 78). From left to right are (first row) Michael Haggard, Charles B. Ecton, 1st Sgt. John A. Gordon, and Joe Ancil Watts; (second row) George Birch, Archie Piersall, Thomas Parris, and 2nd Lt. Thomas Birch. (Orphan Brigade Kinfolk.)

Two old comrades-in-arms posed during a Confederate reunion around 1905. James W. Nelson (left) enlisted in Company F, 4th Kentucky Infantry at Camp Burnett in August 1861. He fought in all the battles of his company and was wounded near Camden, South Carolina in his regiment's final battle in late April 1865. He died at the Kentucky Confederate Home on May 22, 1907, and was buried in the Pewee Valley Confederate Cemetery. James Gaither Bryant served in the same unit with Nelson. He died August 1, 1920, and was buried in the Loy Cemetery in Adair County. (Geoff Walden.)

These Mercer County veterans held a reunion in June 1905. From left to right are (first row) Robert Procter Soper, Joseph Buford Nooe, T. M. Cardwell, Frank Rue, Charles Bonta, J. M. Board, J. G. Hunter, J. O. Dedman, Stephen Woolridge, McClung McAfee, James Parker, ? Stewart, Creth Robinson, Dallas Chinn, and "Daddy" Brooks; (second row) George Fallis, G. N. Handy, John Milburn, Jewett McCoun, unidentified, Jesse Tyler, Smith Hansford, W. J. Hanna, J. D. Bryant, ? Smith, James Woods, Wesley Robards, George Bissick, W. K. Armstrong, Richard Bryant, and J. P. Chinn. (Orphan Brigade Kinfolk.)

Members of the Kentucky Division UCV met for their first annual convention in Louisville on October 22–23, 1901. Gen. James M. Poyntz, commander of the Kentucky Division, noted that the Kentucky UCV had grown to include over 60 camps. The veterans posed for a group photograph on the front steps of the famous Galt House hotel in Louisville. (Orphan Brigade Kinfolk.)

GEN. S. B. BUCKNER
Great Organizer
Became Lt.-Gen.

Gen. John C. Breckinridge
Leader everywhere
Became Major-Gen.

Gen. Ben Hardin Helm
Loved Drill Master
Killed. Chicamauga.

ORPHAN BRIGADE, C. S. A.

Souvenir Program

THURSDAY, SEPTEMBER 24, 1914,
ELIZABETHTOWN, KENTUCKY.

HARDIN COUNTY ORPHAN BRIGADE MEMBERS:

BRIG. GEN.—BEN HARDIN HELM.
COLONEL—MARTIN HARDIN COFER.
MAJOR—THOS. HERCULES HAYS.
MAJOR—G. W. MAXON.
MAJOR—R. C. WINTERSMITH.
CAPTAIN—W. LEE HARNED.
CAPT.—FAYETTE HEWITT, Adjt. Gen.

CAPTAIN—FRANK D. MOFFITT.
LIEUTENANT—E. J. FREEMAN.
LIEUTENANT—R. S. FORD.
LIEUTENANT—JAMES HARGAN.
LIEUTENANT—JAMES CLAY HAYS.
LIEUTENANT—VIRGIL HEWITT, Adjt.
LIEUTENANT—CHAS. H. THOMAS.

(Continued on next page.)

GEN. R. W. HANSON
Disciplinarian
Killed, Murfreesboro.

GEN. JOS. H. LEWIS
Kind Uncle
To Every Man.

The veterans of the Orphan Brigade met in reunion at Elizabethtown, Kentucky, on September 24, 1914. This was the 31st annual reunion of the Orphan Brigade. The veterans had met in Elizabethtown once before, in 1884, for the reinterment of Gen. Ben Hardin Helm in his family cemetery. Helm, who was killed at Chickamauga in September 1863 (see page 28), was initially buried in Atlanta but was brought back home in 1884 and reburied by members of the Orphan Brigade and Helm's original regiment, the 1st Kentucky Cavalry. At this reunion, the surviving members of the 1st Kentucky Cavalry were adopted into the ranks of the Orphan Brigade, and all Kentucky Confederate veterans were invited to participate in their future reunions. The program for the 1914 reunion featured images of the most beloved commanders of the Orphan Brigade, Gen. Simon B. Buckner, Gen. John C. Breckinridge, Gen. Ben Hardin Helm, Gen. Roger W. Hanson, and Gen. Joseph H. Lewis. (Timothy D. Bowman.)

The sixth reunion of the Orphan Brigade was held at Bardstown on August 18, 1887, and was attended by over 250 veterans. The veterans and their families first went to the Bardstown Cemetery, where they were met at the gate by local children with flowers to decorate the graves of Confederate veterans, which was an important part of all Orphan Brigade reunions. The group then gathered at St. Joseph College for their business meeting. The veterans were welcomed to Bardstown by Judge John Fulton, who introduced General Lewis and General Buckner as speakers. The keynote address, a memorial to General Helm, was given at the evening banquet by E. Polk Johnson. Some of the veterans posed for this group picture at the back of one of the college buildings. No identification of all seen in the photograph has been preserved, but the following were seated in chairs in the third row, center, from left to right, Gen. Joseph H. Lewis, Mrs. Roger W. Hanson (Virginia), unidentified, Gen. Simon B. Buckner, and Mrs. Ben Hardin Helm (Emilie Todd). (Geoff Walden.)

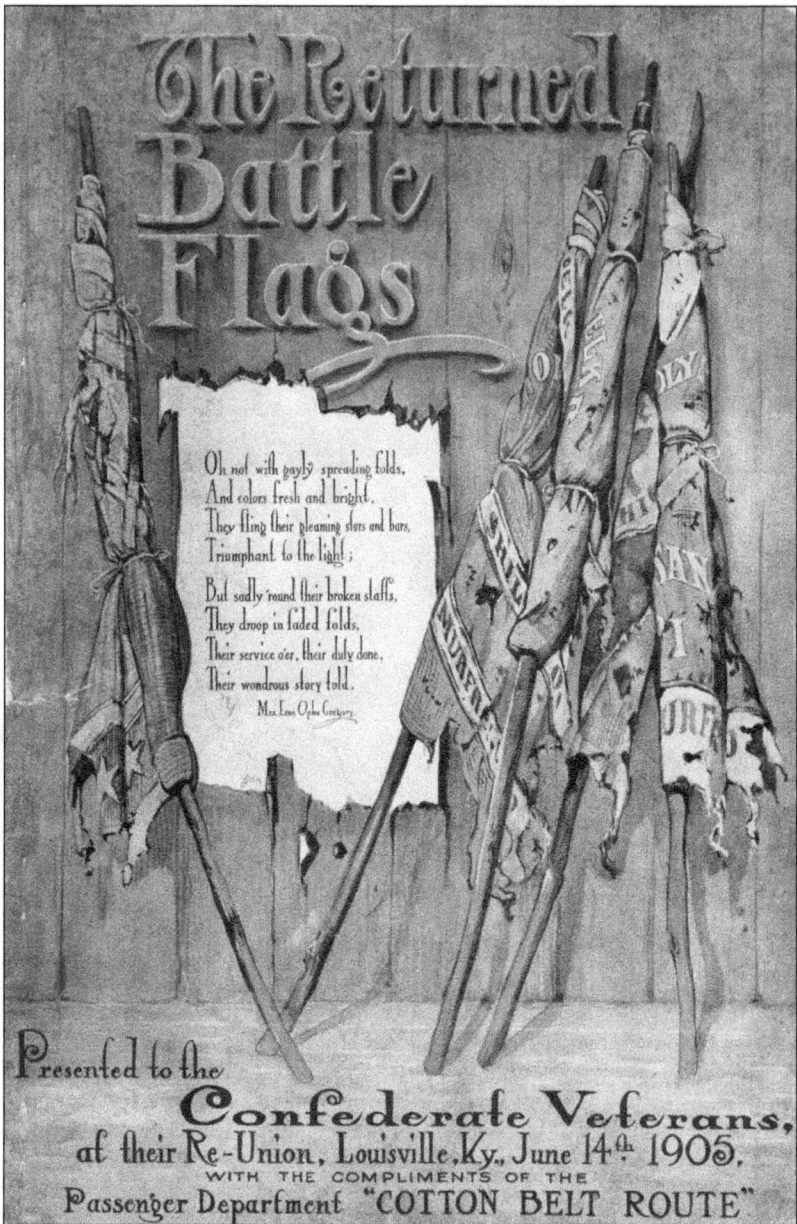

At the grand Confederate veterans reunion in Louisville in June 1905, each veteran was given a small pamphlet that commemorated the return of the captured Confederate battle flags to the South. When an enemy flag was captured by Federal forces, it was supposed to be forwarded to the War Department in Washington. Although many captured Confederate flags were kept by the soldiers or units that captured them and many were sent home to Northern states, those that were sent to Washington were catalogued and retained until March 1905, when they were finally returned to the Southern states. Pres. Grover Cleveland had attempted to return the captured Confederate flags by executive order in 1887, but the Grand Army of the Republic, a group of Union veterans, protested so loudly that Cleveland rescinded his order. Finally, in February 1905, a joint resolution of Congress directed the secretary of war to return the Confederate flags to the Southern states whose units had borne them. (Geoff Walden.)

The battle flag of the 6th Kentucky Infantry was one of those captured flags that were returned to the South in 1905. Issued in January 1864, the flag bore battle honors for Shiloh, Vicksburg, Baton Rouge, Murfreesboro, and Chickamauga, as well as crossed cannons signifying the regiment's capture of artillery at Chickamauga. Seen in this photograph taken about 1920, the flag was still mounted on its original hickory limb staff. (Kentucky Military History Museum.)

These veterans of the 4th and 6th Kentucky Infantry Regiments posed at the grand Confederate reunion in Louisville in June 1905. From left to right are (first row) Dr. Benjamin Bell Scott, 1st Sgt. George Edwards Johnston, Pvt. Theodore Cowherd, and unidentified; (second row) Pvt. James Bell, Pvt. Wilson Pope Perry, Cpl. Ambrose Jackson Hall, Cpl. Holman Hardin Smith (see page 36), and unidentified. (Geoff Walden.)

George H. Mitchell served as a private in Company G, 9th Kentucky Cavalry. One month after enlisting in the Confederate army, he fought his first battle at Perryville, Kentucky, on October 8, 1862. Mitchell returned home in 1865 and died in 1925. He was buried in the Campbellsburg Cemetery in Henry County. While visiting the Chickamauga Battlefield Park in 1911, Mitchell posed for this picture at one of the guns marking the position of Cobb's Kentucky Battery. (Naomi McGrew, Mitchell's granddaughter.)

Members of the Jim Moss Camp 1287 of the UCV met in Arlington, Kentucky, around 1900. From left to right are (first row) William J. Berry, James H. McConnell, Daniel Mosby, Thomas A. McMurray, John E. Berry, Richard Porter, and William Henry McMurray; (second row) T. B. Ellis, Charles Allred, William J. Layton, William J. Sullenger, Joseph C. Berry, James W. Martinie, William E. Dodson, Abel Davis, David Crockett Holder, and Charles V. Knight; (third row) Dr. John R. Owen, James Magruder Ellis, John Wesley Felts, George Clay Anderson, H. Marshall Tibbs, William Seaborn Jackson, John H. Vance, William Jennings, Britt Glenn, and John W. Edwards. (Orphan Brigade Kinfolk.)

Pvt. Daniel Black joined Capt. Robert Cobb's battery of artillery in July 1861. In this photograph taken around 1900, he is seen posing at the gun position he manned during the battle of Chickamauga on September 20, 1863. Black had this photograph taken so he could explain to his relatives why he was shot in the back during the battle. He posed showing his proper stance as part of the gun drill, which required him to turn his back to the muzzle when the cannon was fired. (Rebecca Blackburn and Tom Prince.)

Veterans from Lyon County, most of whom were members of Cobb's Battery, posed for a group photograph at their reunion at Mint Springs, Kuttawa, Kentucky, in 1901. From left to right are Gen. Hylan B. Lyon, who formed Cobb's Battery (see page 91), Lt. Bart James, Cpl. James Darrah, ? Dobbins, Pvt. Frank M. Wadlington, unidentified, Pvt. Newton Payne, Pvt. Daniel Black, Pvt. Daniel Hawley, Mary Jenkins, and Ki Payne. (Julian and Georgette Beatty.)

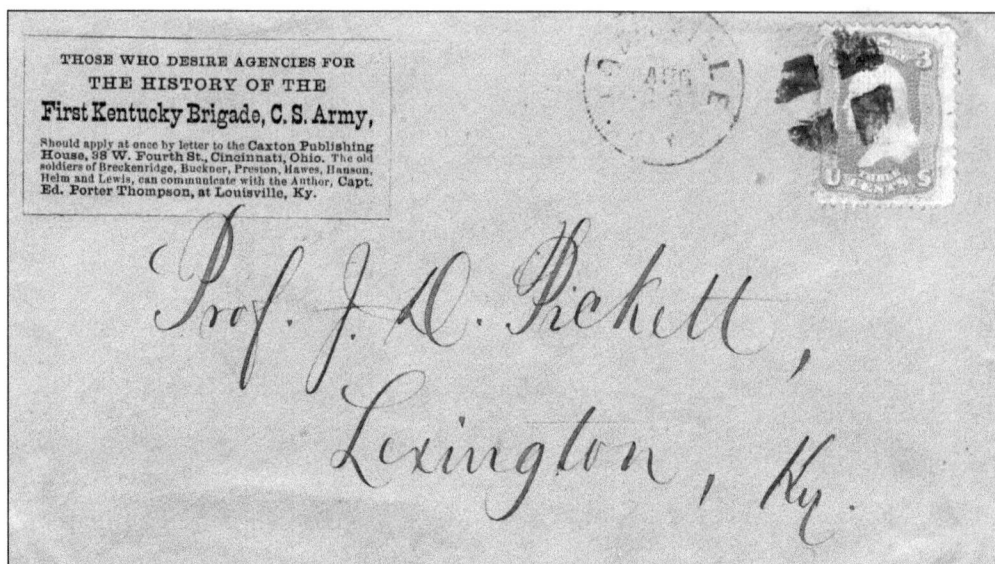

In 1868, Capt. Ed Porter Thompson of the 6th Kentucky Infantry published his first book, *History of the First Kentucky Brigade*. The expanded revision, *History of the Orphan Brigade*, followed in 1898. These two books are considered among the best Confederate unit histories, containing unit rosters, battle and campaign history, and humorous anecdotes. This envelope, advertising the 1868 edition, was mailed to Joseph Desha Pickett of Lexington. (Geoff Walden.)

A native of Mason County, Joseph Desha Pickett served as chaplain of the 2nd Kentucky Infantry and the Orphan Brigade. He was often seen in the midst of enemy fire on the battlefield, and when his friends warned him against the danger, he replied, "Those who need my services first and most are those who fall first in the battles of my country." (*History of the First Kentucky Brigade*, 1868.)

Members of the Walker Camp 640 UCV, seen posing in Greenlawn Cemetery in Franklin in June 1910, are, from left to right, Nicholas Craft Rose, 14th Tennessee Infantry; Wilson Pope Perry, 9th Tennessee Cavalry; Jesse Wilson Baird, 9th Kentucky Infantry; Ped V. Mayes, 30th Tennessee Infantry; James R. Garrett, 1st Georgia Reserves; Josephus C. Bryan, 6th Kentucky Infantry; John L. Rogers, 6th Kentucky Infantry (see page 46); Otho Haydon, 9th Kentucky Infantry; J. William Travis, 6th Kentucky Infantry; and William J. Barnard, 30th Tennessee Infantry. (Octagon Hall Museum.)

Veterans of the Orphan Brigade met in Franklin, Kentucky, in June 1910. An important part of many veteran reunions was visiting the local cemetery to decorate the graves of Confederates who had passed on. These reunion attendees visited the grave of Capt. David C. Walker, 6th Kentucky Infantry, in Greenlawn Cemetery. (Octagon Hall Museum.)

Veterans of Morgan's Men met in reunion at Estill Springs, Kentucky, on August 20–22, 1924. From left to right are (first row) George W. Muir, E. P. Halley, Walter Shropshire, E. A. Allen, J. William Boyd, John E. Abraham, J. Esten Keller, Dan Perrine, M. H. Haggard, Ely Blackburn, George B. Taylor, H. M. Taylor, W. H. Robb, C. H. Meng, Alexander Tribble, Harry Shaw, Samuel Meeks, J. A. Falconer, N. B. Deatherage, James N. Stone, and C. H. Lee Jr.; (second row) A. Gordon Sulser, J. Sherman Porter, David Clarke, E. L. Crystal, James S. Clarke, W. C. Stipp, R. P. Scobee, J. M. Craig, T. D. English, J. H. Baughman, W. H. Tucker, Gano Hildreth, J. B. White, Beriah Magoffin, J. W. Booher, John Milward, and Frank C. Taylor. (Special Collections, University of Kentucky.)

These men were prisoners of war with Gen. John Hunt Morgan in the Ohio State Penitentiary in 1863. From left to right are (first row) D. H. James, Robert Berry, Col. Cicero Coleman, Ben B. Bigstaff, Col. W. C. P. Breckinridge, Robert S. Bullock, and Richard Curd Morgan; (second row) P. H. Eastin, L. P. Young, O. F. Redd, George B. Taylor, R. M. Redd, J. R. Morton, C. F. Estill, Alexander W. Macklin, R. K. Byrnes, and H. R. Engman. (Special Collections, University of Kentucky.)

The Kentucky Confederate Soldiers Home was established at Pewee Valley in 1902 and operated for 32 years. At its height, over 350 veterans had been admitted to the home, where their meals and daily needs were provided by the staff. Many of the old soldiers were buried in the nearby Pewee Valley Confederate Cemetery, which holds the graves of over 300 Confederate veterans. (*Confederate Veteran Magazine*, 1902.)

Martin Vanburen Dyer was born in Breckinridge County on May 4, 1837. He enlisted in September 1861 in Company G, 9th Kentucky Infantry, and fought in most of the engagements of his company. Later in life, he lived at the Kentucky Confederate Home at Pewee Valley, where he was awarded the Southern Cross of Honor. Dyer is buried in Lewisport, Kentucky. (Rod Halsey, Dyer's great-great grandson.)

James A. McDonald (right) of Paris, Kentucky, poses with the restored battle flag of his regiment in 1925. This flag was first carried by the 1st Kentucky Infantry in 1861, then it was transferred to the 2nd Kentucky Infantry when they were exchanged after the surrender of Fort Donelson in 1862. The flag was returned to Paris in 1924, where it was restored and is now on display in the Hopewell Museum. (*Confederate Veteran Magazine*, 1925.)

Relatives of Bettie Taylor Phillips pose with the battle flag of the 4th Kentucky Infantry in 1915. This flag pattern of a dark blue field with a red cross was issued to the units under General Breckinridge's command in the spring or summer of 1862. At the end of the war, Mrs. Phillips, who had accompanied her husband to the battle area, brought this flag back to Kentucky. It is preserved today in the Kentucky Military History Museum in Frankfort. (Waveland State Historic Site.)

Born in 1837, Martin Vanburen Dyer served in the "Breckinridge Grays," Company G, 9th Kentucky Infantry. He entered the Kentucky Confederate Home in 1906 and lived there until his death in 1909. This photograph and the one on page 111 show Dyer in his veteran's uniform at the Pewee Valley Home. (Rod Halsey, Dyer's great-great grandson.)

4803. Confederate Home, Pewee Valley, Louisville, Ky.

Founded in 1902 by Bennett Young and others, the Kentucky Confederate Home at Pewee Valley served over 700 Confederate veterans during its history. Although much of the home burned in 1920, a wing survived and was large enough to house the remaining occupants, and the home remained in operation until 1934, when only five veterans remained. (Geoff Walden.)

Theodore Cowherd was born in Taylor County in 1844. He enlisted in Company F, 4th Kentucky Infantry and fought in all the battles of his company. He was wounded at Shiloh and Resaca. During the Battle of Atlanta, Cowherd was severely wounded, and his right arm was amputated. His empty right sleeve can be seen in this photograph taken at a reunion in 1905. Cowherd died in 1920 and was buried in Cave Hill Cemetery in Louisville. (Geoff Walden.)

Born in 1843, Bennett Henderson Young was one of the most daring Kentucky Confederates. He was captured in 1863 but escaped from Camp Douglas, Illinois, into Canada. On October 19, 1864, Young and some compatriots pulled one of the most remarkable attacks of the war when they raided St. Albans, Vermont, robbing the local banks and setting fire to some buildings. After the war, Young was elected commander of the United Confederate Veterans. (Orphan Brigade Kinfolk.)

Five

MONUMENTS TO
THEIR MEMORY

Lexington hosted a large celebration on October 18, 1911, when the United Daughters of the Confederacy unveiled an equestrian monument to revered cavalry leader John Hunt Morgan before a crowd of some 25,000. Controversy arose when sculptor Pompeo Coppini chose to depict a stallion, even though Morgan's favorite horse, Black Bess, was a mare. (Library of Congress.)

GEN. JOHN C. BRECKINRIDGE MONUMENT, LEXINGTON, KY.—13

Lexington native Gen. John C. Breckinridge was honored with a statue on the lawn of the Fayette County Courthouse erected by the Commonwealth of Kentucky in 1887. Breckinridge is shown leaning on a draped column with his hand outstretched, signifying his years of public service. The postcard view shown here was dated 1947. (Geoff Walden.)

Busts of several Confederate generals from Kentucky grace Kentucky Avenue in the Vicksburg National Military Park. Gen. John C. Breckinridge commanded forces in Mississippi in the summers of 1862 and 1863, and his Kentucky Orphan Brigade manned the Vicksburg trenches in defense of the city in July 1862. (Geoff Walden.)

The most imposing Confederate monument in Kentucky is the obelisk erected at the birthplace of Confederate president Jefferson Davis at Fairview in Todd County. This 351-foot shaft is the tallest concrete obelisk in the world. Completed in 1924, the monument features an elevator that carries visitors to the top for a grand view of the Kentucky countryside. (Geoff Walden.)

JEFFERSON DAVIS MONUMENT, HEIGHT 351 FEET, COST $265,000

FAIRVIEW, HIGHWAY 68, NEAR HOPKINSVILLE, KY.—12

Gen. Ben Hardin Helm, beloved commander of the Kentucky Orphan Brigade, is honored with a statue on Kentucky Avenue in the Vicksburg National Military Park in Mississippi. His men helped defend Vicksburg in 1862, and some volunteers even served on the Confederate ironclad CSS *Arkansas* in its battles against the Union river fleet. (Geoff Walden.)

117

The Confederate monument in Madisonville, Hopkins County, was dedicated on May 28, 1909. Gen. Bennett Young, commander of the UCV, addressed a crowd of some 10,000 spectators who held a large portrait of Gen. John C. Breckinridge. Ten-year-old Marvene Cunningham, granddaughter of veteran Thomas Burton Jones, can be seen placing a wreath at the corner of the monument. (Sue Russell, daughter of Marvene Cunningham.)

The Paris Cemetery in Bourbon County boasts this limestone pillar that was dedicated to the memory of Bourbon County's Confederates in 1887. Confederate veterans buried near the monument include Pvt. James McDonald of the 2nd Kentucky Infantry (see page 112) and Capt. William Bramblett of the 4th Kentucky Infantry (see page 25). (Special Collections, University of Kentucky.)

One of the best-known Confederate monuments in Kentucky is located in Louisville, near the campus of the University of Louisville. It was erected by the Kentucky Women's Confederate Monument Association in 1895. The 70-foot-tall monument features an 8-foot-tall bronze infantryman with his musket in hand and other figures representing the artillery and cavalry. This postcard view is dated 1913. (Geoff Walden.)

4582.   Confederate Monument, Louisville, Ky.

Thought to be the oldest Confederate monument in Kentucky, this marble shaft stands in Battle Grove Cemetery in Cynthiana. The monument was dedicated on May 27, 1869, in memory of the Confederate dead who fell in defense of constitutional liberty. This memorial stands in the center of a circle of 47 Confederate graves marking the casualties of the battles at Cynthiana in 1862 and 1864. (Geoff Walden.)

Kentucky State Monument,
Chickamauga Park,
Chattanooga, Tenn.

On May 3, 1899, Kentucky dedicated a monument to its soldiers who fought in the battle of Chickamauga, Georgia, in September 1863. Maj. Thomas H. Hays of the Kentucky Commission, formerly of the 6th Kentucky Infantry (see page 35), presented the monument to Kentucky governor William Bradley. The monument honors both blue and gray soldiers from Kentucky, who fought one another at Chickamauga. (Geoff Walden.)

This brass badge was a souvenir of the dedication of the Kentucky and Georgia Confederate monuments on the Chickamauga battlefield, May 3–4, 1899. The badge features a depiction of the Kentucky monument, which stands on ground where soldiers from the 4th and 6th Kentucky Infantry regiments CSA and soldiers from the 15th Kentucky Infantry USA met in battle on September 20, 1863. (Gary Gardner.)

Copyright 1906 by the Rotograph Co.

G 17048 Confederate Monument. Frankfort, Ky.

The Confederate Soldier Monument in the Frankfort Cemetery was erected in 1892 amidst a circle of graves of Confederate soldiers who had been killed in the battle of Chickamauga in September 1863. These Kentucky soldiers were originally buried on or near the battlefield, but they were removed in 1888 and reinterred in Frankfort. The circle also contains the graves of four soldiers who had been executed in Kentucky by Union authorities. (Geoff Walden.)

Two Confederate monuments stand near each other in the Lexington Cemetery. The marble soldier was erected in 1893, and the unique monument seen in the background of this early-20th-century photograph was erected in 1874. It features a motif of a Confederate flag hanging from a broken flagstaff and leaning against a log cross. (Special Collections, University of Kentucky.)

121

One of the most unusual monuments in Kentucky is this rock obelisk near Horse Cave, which marks the grave of an unknown soldier from Louisiana who was killed in an accident on September 9, 1862, while advancing as part of General Bragg's army. Landowner Sam Lively erected the monument in 1934, and it still stands today. (Hart County Historical Society.)

Gen. George Blake Cosby of Louisville commanded a brigade of Kentucky cavalry troops in central Mississippi in the summer of 1863. His brigade served under Gen. Earl Van Dorn and Gen. Joseph Johnston, who attempted to relieve the besieged city of Vicksburg. This monument is located on Kentucky Avenue in the Vicksburg National Military Park. (Geoff Walden.)

The Confederate monument in Danville honors Capt. Robert D. Logan of the 6th Kentucky Cavalry, who had been one of the "Immortal 600" Confederate prisoners of war. The marble soldier on the top of the monument is a portrait of Captain Logan, who was one of the most admired veterans in Boyle County when he died in 1896. See page 67. (Geoff Walden.)

John Breckinridge Castleman of Louisville, a fearless Confederate cavalry leader during the war, was a champion horseman and leader of the American Saddlebred Horse Association in later life. This bronze statue, erected in Louisville's Cherokee Triangle in 1913, honors his Confederate service, equestrian achievements, and service in the U.S. Army during the Spanish-American War. See page 90. (Geoff Walden.)

For many years, a large white oak tree known as the "Zollie Tree" formed a living Confederate monument on the Mill Springs battlefield in Pulaski County. Gen. Felix Zollicoffer and some 150 of his soldiers were killed in battle here on January 19, 1862. Local girl Dorotha Burton decorated the Zollie Tree annually with a wreath of evergreens, and news of this homegrown memorial encouraged the placement of Confederate markers in 1910. (Mill Springs Battlefield Association.)

This monument in Zollicoffer Park near Nancy, Kentucky, honors the Confederate soldiers who fell in the battle of Mill Springs (Fishing Creek). The rough-hewn shaft was erected in 1910 by a committee headed by Gen. Bennett Young, commander of the UCV. A nearby memorial marker stands on one of the Confederate mass graves on the battlefield. (Geoff Walden.)

The largest Civil War battle in Kentucky was fought near Perryville on October 8, 1862. Although the Confederates gained a tactical victory, gathering Union reinforcements forced Gen. Braxton Bragg to retreat, ending his invasion of Kentucky. This monument honoring the Confederates killed in the battle, numbering about 530, was erected in 1902 at the site of one of the mass graves on the battlefield. (Perryville State Historic Site.)

The Sons of Confederate Veterans keep the memory of Kentucky's Confederate soldiers alive by erecting monuments and historical markers, marking the graves of Confederate soldiers and other educational and preservation activities. The 730 members of the Kentucky Division SCV have performed tasks such as erecting 150 Confederate grave markers at Zollicoffer Park. (Geoff Walden.)

BIBLIOGRAPHY

Confederate Home Messenger. Journal of the Kentucky Confederate Home (Pewee Valley, KY) 1907–1911.

Confederate Veteran Association of Kentucky. Fifth Edition. Lexington: Transylvania Printing Co., 1895.

Davis, William C. *The Orphan Brigade: The Kentucky Confederates Who Couldn't Go Home.* New York: Doubleday, 1980.

Duke, Basil W. *A History of Morgan's Cavalry.* West Jefferson, OH: Genesis Publishing Co., 1997.

Johnson, Adam R., and William J. Davis, ed. *The Partisan Rangers of the Confederate States Army.* Louisville: Geo. G. Fetter Company, 1904.

Kentucky Adjutant General's Office. *Report of the Adjutant General of the State of Kentucky: Confederate Kentucky Volunteers, War 1861–1865.* Frankfort, KY: State Journal Company Printers, 1915–1918.

Lynn, Stephen Douglas, *Confederate Pensioners of Kentucky.* Baltimore: Gateway Press, Inc., 2000.

———. *Confederate Soldiers of Kentucky.* Lexington: Self-published, 2002.

Ramage, James A. *Rebel Raider: The Life of General John Hunt Morgan.* Lexington: University Press of Kentucky, 1986.

Southern Bivouac Magazine (Louisville) 1882–1885.

Thompson, Ed Porter. *History of the First Kentucky Brigade.* Cincinnati: Caxton Publishing House, 1868.

———. *History of the Orphan Brigade.* Louisville: Lewis N. Thompson, 1898.

INDEX

This index is not comprehensive but lists most subjects that appear more than once.

Visit us at
arcadiapublishing.com

www.ingramcontent.com/pod-product-compliance
Lightning Source LLC
Chambersburg PA
CBHW050544110426
42813CB00008B/2253